THE CHRONLOGY OF ANCIENT INDIA

THE CHRONLOGY OF ANCIENT INDIA

VELANDAI GOPALA AIYER

GYAN

Published by

Gyan Publishing House
5, Ansari Road
Daryaganj, New Delhi-110002
Phone: 011-47034999, 9811692060
E-mail: books@gyanbooks.com

Distribution Network
gyanbooks.com
India, USA, Canada, UK, Australia

ISBN: 978-93-7169-383-7 (PB)

First Published, 1901

2nd Impression 2025

Printed at: Gyan Press, Delhi.

THE CHRONLOGY OF ANCIENT INDIA
Author: VELANDAI GOPALA AIYER

The Chronology of Ancient India

First Series.
- The Beginning of the Kali Yuga
- The Date of the Mahabharata War
- The Four Yugas

BY

VELANDAI GOPALA AIYER, B.A.,

PLEADER, CHITTOOR.

Madras:

G. A. NATESAN & Co., PUBLISHERS, ESPLANADE.

1901.

PREFACE.

IN this small volume, * I have endeavoured to present to the public a part of the results of an impartial enquiry, conducted by me during the last six years, into a few leading questions concerning the Chronology of Ancient India. In carrying out, however inadequately, so important a task, I have been helped to a large extent by the laborious researches of many erudite scholars, whose names and writings are noticed in appropriate places in the body of the work and to every one of whom I am extremely grateful. This part fixes the date of the most important event in the Ancient History of India,—the great Mahabharata War. Once this is known, the limits of the Vedic period preceding, and of the Epic period succeeding, it, are easily ascertainable. The Third chapter endeavours to give a rational explanation of the Yugas. A glance at the Table of Contents will reveal the many topics of interest and importance incidentally discussed, such as the following:—the identification of Bharani 10°, as given by the Vedanga Jyotisha, with the beginning of the Krittikas, the deduction of chronological particulars from the statements of Clas-

* These papers originally appeared in the *Indian Review*.

sical writers, a rational account of the history of the Kollam Andu, and a critical examination of the chronological data of the Rajatarangini.

The second part, which in all probability will be issued before the middle of next year, will first show how the Kaliyuga which really began in 1177 B. C. came subsequently to be supposed to have commenced in 3102 B.C., and will discuss the date of the Vishnu Purana, the astronomical explanation of the Yugas and the nature of the epochs and cycles prevalent in India. The next chapter, perhaps the most important in the whole book, will attempt to place the date of the Rigveda beyond all reasonable doubt by a discussion of certain passages in that Veda, hitherto misunderstood, which yield us, not vague generalisations or bare possibilities, but specific unimpeachable testimony. The concluding chapter will examine further fresh materials, fix the date of the Aryan immigration into India and close with a short *resume* of the leading facts in the History of Aryan India from the earliest times to the sixth century after Christ, such of the few footprints as can still be traced in the shifting sands of Time.

CHITTOOR,
November 28, 1901.

V. GOPALA AIYER.

CONTENTS.

CHAPTER I.

THE BEGINNING OF THE KALIYUGA.

CHAPTER II.

THE DATE OF THE MAHABHARATA WAR.

CHAPTER III.

THE FOUR YUGAS.

The Chronology of Ancient India.

CHAPTER I.

THE BEGINNING OF THE KALIYUGA.

THE heroes of the Mahabharata War and the chief incidents connected therewith are matters almost of daily conversation even in the remotest corners of India. In most of the Indian villages the wars are fought over again and again in the rude, but powerful, nightlong dramatic performances. The most illiterate villager of the poorest hamlet knows, or thinks he knows, something of the great Pandava heroes. The annual Dharmaraja festivals serve to freshen his untrained memory and to stir up his dormant feelings. The cultured Brahman, on the other hand, who piously recites, day after day, portions of the Bhagavad Gita, that marvellous episode in the great Indian epic, is daily reminded of that great conflict which ushered in the modern or the Kali Age. Yet, educated India cares seldom to enquire into the question of the date of the War with even a little of that historical spirit which above everything else distinguishes the European from the Hindu.

Not that materials are wanting to guide us in our attempts to arrive at the truth. Nor is it even that Hindus of requisite ability and knowledge are loath to tackle such problems, a solution of which would be most heartily welcomed by every lover of India. Rather it is that false pride which refuses to question long-cherished opinions and which feels greater pleasure in treating events as of the remotest antiquity. Sometimes it is that new-fangled mysticism which aims at giving impossible explanations of every pre-existing opinion or prejudice. When the atmosphere is so ill-suited, the light of history cannot illuminate the dark labyrinthian passages of the Ancient Chronology of India. What India is now in need of is that faculty of scientific intuition which should divest itself of any tendency that might stand in the way of historical veracity. It is the humble purpose of the writer to dispassionately discuss such materials as may be forthcoming, in order to draw therefrom certain conclusions respecting the date of the War and the chronology of Ancient India.

The date of the war is, as is well known, mixed up with the system of Yugas about which many learned scholars have hitherto written. The present Yuga began soon after the great war was fought in the holy plains of Kurukshetra; and if it be possible to arrive even approximately at the date of the War, the riddle of the Yugas, which has hitherto baffled the ingenuity of learned scholars, will have been in a manner solved.

Was the War an historical event or is it a mere allegory? Almost all scholars * are agreed that a great War took place between the Kurus and the Panchalas very long before Gautama Buddha was born. They have no doubt that the epic narrates truly, though rather extravagantly, a war that waged with disastrous results in the northern parts of India. "There can be little doubt," says Professor Macdonell, "that the original kernel of the epic has, as an historical background, an ancient conflict between the two neighbouring tribes of the Kurus and the Panchalas who finally coalesced into a single people."† Lassen ‡ thought that the epic narrated an actual conflict between the Kurus and the Panchalas, the latter under the leadership of the Pandavas, ending in their mutual annihilation. Weber§ says that "one thing is clearly discernible in

*R. C. Dutt's Civilisation in Ancient India, Vol. I page 10. Weber's Indian Literature, page 187.

† Sanskrit Literature, 285.

‡ Weber's Indian Literature, 135.

§ Weber's Indian Literature, page 187.

the Mahabharata, that it has as its basis a War waged on the soil of Hindustan between Aryan tribes and therefore belonging probably to a time when their settlement in India and the subjugation and Brahmanisation of the native inhabitants, had already been accomplished." It may be idle at this late hour to establish by arguments what has been already conceded by scholars that the main plot of our epic is based on history. It is an easy pastime to deny the truth of the events of the past: but strangely enough it is often difficult to prove their actual occurrence. Did not the late Archbishop Whately, the famous logician, prove conclusively that the great Napoleon had never existed? Yet, that hero of many fights it was that more than anybody else shaped the fortunes, and altered the map, of many a country in the dawn of the century that has now expired. The lesson that the learned divine so humorously teaches must not, by us, be lost sight of in dealing with the new order of sceptical critics whose erratic genius takes the greatest pleasure in denying the fundamental basis of the Sanskrit epic, in whose truth nearly a seventh of the human race sincerely believes.

Nor are the chief characters and the principal incidents of the War merely poetic fictions. It is ridiculous to suppose that an epic with such strong characterisation could be a fabrication of an ingenious mind, at any rate, in India. It needs not much knowledge of Sanskrit literature to discover that the heroes and the heroines of standard Indian works are almost all of the same type. The tameness of similarity is a standing reproach against Sanskrit dramatic literature. But as for the Mahabharata, what wealth of characterisation, what artistic delicacy of touch, what depth of human interest, all depicted in the most natural manner and without the slightest appearance of effort! "In the Mahabharata human interest everywhere preponderates, and a number of well-defined personages are introduced, to whom the possibility of historical existence cannot be denied."* The high-souled Karna, for instance, loyal and generous, but vain and boastful; Yudhishtira, the good and the wise, but fond of dice whose dangers he had the intelligence to understand, but whose temptations he had not the strength of will to resist; the lion-hearted Bhima, righteous but vindictive; the chivalrous Arjuna and the cultured Sahadeva; the politic Sri Krishna and the downright Balarama; the Royal sage Bhishma and the Brahman warrior Drona; the impetuous Asvathaman; the envious Duryodhana and the unprincipled Sakuni; the

* Weber's Indian Literature, page 192.

imperious Droupadi and the faithful Gandhari;—every one of these so unlike every other. There is no attempt in all Sanskrit literature at such matchless character painting. But the epic is based on a substratum of historical facts and therefore successfully accomplishes what no other work in all India has ever attempted. Visakhadatta's Mudrarakshasa is indeed a feeble exception, but here again the plot is borrowed from real history.

Furthermore, let a traveller pass through any tract in India from the Himalayas to the Cape, from Kathiawar to Burma; he is confronted everywhere with striking evidence that the Pandava princes are still held in the deepest veneration by the Brahman and the Jain, by the cultured races of the plains and the primitive tribes of the hills. The influence of a got-up poem may affect the literate classes, but not the simple rustics inhabiting hilly isolated regions. Unless the main events of the war had actually taken place, the influence of an imaginary epic, however grand and however thrilling, cannot take the leading place in the hearts of the untutored millions of India.

It is well known that the five Pandava heroes married a single maiden, the Panchala Droupadi. "The description of the transaction represents it as one which was opposed to public opinion and which was justified more by very remote tradition than by existing practice."* The epic represents Drupada, the father of the lady, as having been shocked at the proposal of all the princes marrying his daughter. Undoubtedly, as Professor Max Muller† remarked, the epic tradition must have been very strong to compel the author to record a proceeding so violently opposed to Brahmanical law. If the characters and the incidents of the epic were purely mythical, how comes it that the compilers thereof thought it proper to give special prominence to such an un-Aryan practice?

In the oldest of the Vedas the names of the two royal brothers Devapi and Santanu are mentioned, the latter of whom was the great grandfather of the Pandavas and the Kauravas. In the Aitareya Brahmana and in the Satapatha Brahmana, Janamejaya Parikshita, the great grandson of Pandava Arjuna, is mentioned, and from the latter work we may also gather that Janamejaya and his three brothers, Bhimasena, Ugrasena and Srutasena, had died shortly before its compilation. Professor Weber‡ says that in the Kathaka Samhita, a Sakha of the Black Yajurveda, mention is made of Dhritarashtra Vaichitravirya and the contests of the Pan-

* J. D. Mayne's Hindu Law and Usage p. 65.

† Ancient Sanskrit Literature, p. 46.

‡ Indische Studien, III. p. 469—472.

chalas and the Kounteyas. The Taittiriya Aranyaka mentions Vyasa Parasarya and his pupil Vaisampayana, the former of whom was the actual father of Pandu and Dhritarashtra; and the family of the Parasaras is mentioned with especial frequency in the Vamsas of the White Yajus. Parasara and probably also his son Krishna (Vyasa) are the authors of a few hymns of the Rigveda. The Aswalayana and the Sankhayana Sutras and Panini mention the words 'Bharata' and 'Mahabharata'. Panini, 'who cannot be assigned to a date later than the fourth century B. C.,' and whom Goldstucker places in the ninth or tenth century B. C., speaks of Kunti, Yudhishtira, Vasudeva, Arjuna, and Drona, all of them leading characters in our epic. Dion Chrysostom of the first century A. D. actually speaks of the existence of an Indian Homer; and Patanjali, who lived in the second century B. C., quotes a few verses which are still to be found in the Mahabharata. As all these ancient works and authors bear testimony to the reality of the principal personages that figured in the War, we may consequently conclude that it was an undoubted historical event.

Not only the Mahabharata, but most of the Puranas also, refer to this great War between the Kauravas and the Pandavas. These Puranas are collections of bardic traditions preserved in a systematic manner. Though mainly prophetic in tone, (for it has to be remembered that their reputed author Vyasa Parasarya lived at the time of the war, but the events related therein reach down to a comparatively modern period), they are the repositories of traditional learning and old time legends. Much of what is contained therein has not any historical value; but enough is still to be found in the more authentic ones to attract the attention of the student of history. In the words of the late Mr. H. H. Wilson, 'a very large portion of the contents of many, some portion of the contents of all, is genuine and old; and it is therefore as idle as it is irrational to dispute the antiquity or authenticity of the greater portion of the contents of these Puranas.' They 'contain political and chronological particulars to which on the score of probability there is nothing to object. In fact their general accuracy has been incontrovertibly established.'* The Chandogya Upanishad refers to Itihasa Puranas as a branch of literature; and the Satapatha Brahmana mentions Itihasas and Puranas. May we not infer therefrom that some kind of annals of kings and dynasties existed even in that ancient period? 'Proba-

* Wilson's Vishnu Purana, Introduction.

bly,' says Mr. R. C. Dutt, 'such annals were preserved in the traditions of the people and altered, recast and mixed up with legends from century to century, until after about two thousand years they finally assumed the shape in which we now find them,—the modern Puranas.'*

The Puranas are supposed to treat of the following five subjects: (1) Primary creation or cosmogony; (2) Secondary creation or the destruction and renovation of worlds including chronology; (3) Genealogy of gods and patriarchs; (4) Reigns of the Manus or periods called Manvantaras; and (5) History or such particulars as have been preserved of the ancient dynasties of India. Of the eighteen principal Puranas, the Vishnu, the Vayu, the Matsya, the Bhagavata and the Brahmanda give lists of 'the future kings in Kali'; and these rank, in importance and priority, in the order in which they are named.

The central idea of some of these Puranas and of the astronomical Siddhantas is that the Mahabarata war occurred a few years before 3102 B. C., the supposed beginning of the present Kaliyuga. Though it may be heresy to doubt the truth of this supposition, the least critical mind will find sufficient testimony in the very

* Ancient India, Vol. II p. 29.

same Puranas to controvert this fondly cherished view. The Vishnu Purana states that 1015 years elapsed from the birth of Parikshit to the coronation of Mahapadma Nanda. The Vayu and the Matsya give 1050 years, and the Bhagavata 1115 years, for the interval. They all agree, however, that the Nandas reigned in all for a period of one hundred years. The Vishnu being the least extravagant, a few scholars have been led to believe that 1015 + 100 or 1115 years elapsed between the Mahabharata war, when the birth of Parikshit took place, and the accession to the throne of Chandragupta, the immediate successor of the Nandas. The date of Chandragupta has been incontrovertibly fixed with the aid derived from Greek sources by the unanimous consent of all orientalists at 315 B. C., a date which the late lamented Professor Max Muller rightly called 'the sheet anchor of Indian chronology.'* Consequently the war, which took place 1115 years before Chandragupta's accession, is placed at 1430 B. C. Besides, according to an old method of reckoning, the constellation of the Saptarshis (Ursa Major) was believed to move from one Nakshatra to another in a hundred years and the Puranas relate that the Saptarshis, which were in

* Max Muller's Ancient Sanskrit Literature. p. 298.

Magha Nakshatra at the birth of Parikshit, had moved on to Purvashada Nakshatra at the accession of Nanda to the throne. As there are ten lunar asterisms between Magha and Purvashada, the period denoted by the movement is one thousand years; and the Nandas reigned for a hundred years. Therefore the war is placed 1100 years before Chandragupta, or at about 1415 B. C. Moreover, the vernal equinox was in the beginning of the Krittikas (Pleiades) during the time of the war. As it had receded by reason of the precession of the equinoxes to the Aswini Nakshatra in the year 499 A. D., the war is said to have taken place about 1426 B C. It is also considered that the names Rohineya, Maghabhu, Ashadhabhava, and Purvaphalgunibhava accorded respectively to Mercury, Venus, Mars and Jupiter point to B. C. 1424, when the moon and the planets were in conjunction in the constellations denoted by the names. There is not much force in this last argument, because the positions given in the Vayu and Linga Puranas for some of the planets are totally different. Professor Max Muller is of opinion that "these names of the planets have never been met with either in the Vedas or in any of the early productions."* Besides, there is

* Rig Veda Vol IV. Preface, p. xxxiii.

nothing that connects these positions with the date of the war.

Such are the arguments which are advanced to fix the date of the war in the middle of the fifteenth century B. C.* But Mr. R. C. Dutt and Mr. Fergusson place the war in the middle and in the beginning of the thirteenth century B.C.† respectively. The late Mr. H. H. Wilson thus sums up the opinions of his time on the subject: "According to Col. Wilford's computations (Asiatic Researches Vol. IX, chronological table, p. 116) the conclusion of the great war took place B.C. 1370. Buchanan conjectures it to have occurred in the thirteenth century B.C. Vyasa was the putative father of Pandu and Dhritarashtra and consequently was contemporary with the heroes of the great war. Mr. Colebrooke infers from astronomical data that the arrangement of the Vedas, attributed to Vyasa, took place in the fourteenth century B. C. Mr. Bentley brings the date of Yudhishtira, the chief of the Pandavas, to 575 B. C.; but the weight of authority is in favour of the thirteenth or fourteenth century B. C. for the war of the Mahabharata and the reputed commencement of

* Mr. M. Rangacharya's Yugas, pp. 31-35.

† Dutt's Ancient India, p. 10. Fergusson's History of Indian and Eastern Architecture, p. 36.

the Kali age."* Professor Macdonell traces "the historical germ of the great epic to a very early period which cannot well be later than the tenth century B. C."† While these conflicting opinions are of great value as being indicative of the period when the war might have taken place, they unfortunately lack that precision and certainty which are so much to be desired. It will appear from the sequel that the reasons on which these opinions are based are far from conclusive and that the weight of probability rather indicates a somewhat different date.

To begin with, we have the evidence of the Vedanga Jyotisha, the earliest of the treatises on astronomy to be found in India. A Jyotisha Vedanga is referred to by Apastamba whom Dr. Buhler‡ places on linguistic grounds in the third century B. C. and on other grounds about two centuries still earlier. The Mundakopanishad,§ one of the few ancient Upanishads turned to account in so early a work as the Vedanta Sutras of Badarayana, mentions the six Vedangas by name, of which the Jyotisha is one. We have no means of

* 'Vishnu Purana' Vol. IV. p. 232.

† Sanskrit Literature, p. 285.

‡ Sacred Books of the East, Vol II. Introduction.

§ Mundaka Upanishad I. i. 5

ascertaining whether the Jyotisha known to us as Vedanga is, or is not, the one referred to in those ancient works; but the archaic language in which our Vedanga is written and the unintelligible nature of some of the verses prove beyond doubt that it is a very ancient treatise, though perhaps not as old as the astronomical positions it indicates. The ancient Aryans in India had a knowledge of elementary astronomical phenomena as is evident from the numerous references to them in the Rik and the other Vedas. To better enable them to fix the seasons for their innumerable sacrifices, they devised a few elementary treatises on astronomy, one of which is still preserved to us in the Vedanga Jyotisha. Says Dr. M. Haug in his introduction to his Aitareya Brahmana,* "A regulation of the calendar by such observations was an absolute necessity for the Brahmans; for the proper time of commencing and ending their sacrifices, principally the so-called *sattras* or sacrificial sessions could not be known without an accurate knowledge of the time of the sun's northern and southern progress. The knowledge of the calendar forms such an essential part of the ritual that many important conditions of the latter cannot be carried out without the former." Professor Max Muller admits that there

* Vol I. p. 46.

must have been a real tradition which formed the basis of the astronomical positions recorded in the Vedanga Jyotisha.* It states that the winter solstice occurred with the sun in the beginning of Dhanishta and that the summer solstice took place with the sun in the middle of Aslesha.† Consequently the vernal and autumnal equinoxes occurred with the sun in the end of the third *pada* of Bharani and in the end of the first *pada* of Visakha respectively. We do not find in the Vedanga any division of the ecliptic into360 degrees; this is but natural, because in those early times such scientific divisions could not have been known. The treatise is familiar with the division of the heavens into twenty-seven Nakshatras and probably also with the division of each Nakshatra into four Amsas or quarters. Indeed this old kind of the division of a Nakshatra into four Amsas is referred to in the following slokas of the Vishnu Purana, II. 8:—

प्रथमे कृत्तिके भागे यदा भास्वान्तदा शशी ।
विशाखानां चतुर्थांशे मुने तिष्ठत्यसंशयं ॥
विशाखानां यदा सूर्यश्चरत्यंशं तृतीयकं ।
तदाचंद्रं विजानीयात्कृत्तिका शिरसि स्यितं ।
तदैव विषुवाख्यो वै कालः पुण्योऽभिधीयते ॥

* Rig Veda Vol. IV Preface, p. XXVI.

† Vedanga Jyotisha (Yajur recension), v. 7.

"When the sun, O Sage, is in the first quarter of Krittika and the moon is in the fourth quarter of Visakha, or when the sun is in the third quarter of Visakha and the moon is in the head of Krittika, that is the time of the equinox and it is holy." Mr. Wilson seems to have misunderstood the meaning of भाग and अंश in the above verses, for he takes them to mean 'degree'. It will readily appear that 'quarter' is the more appropriate meaning, for it is only then that the sun and the moon are in "opposition" to each other.

The positions given by the Vedanga Jyotisha are also referred to by Garga* and Varahamihira†; but they differ from those obtaining at present and even from the positions mentioned by Varahamihira as having been observed about the year 3600 ‡ of the modern astronomical Kali era, or in 499 A.D. This great astronomer, who was born in 505 A. D., says in his Brihat Samhita:—"In the old treatises it is said that the summer and winter solstices took place with the sun in the middle of Aslesha and in the beginning of Dhanishta respectively; but *at present* they occur in the beginning of Cancer (beginning of the last quarter of Punarvasu) and

* See Mr. Tilak's Orion, p. 36.

† Brihat Samhita, III. 1 & 2.

‡ Warren's Kala Sankalita, p. 389.

of Capricorn (beginning of the second quarter of Uttarashada) respectively." Therefore the winter solstice, which happened with the sun in the beginning of Dhanishta at the time denoted by the Vedanga, had receded in 499 A.D. to the end of the first quarter of Uttarashada, that is, by an arc of 23.° 20′. As the rate of precession of the equinoxes is, according to the illustrious French savant M. Le Verrier, about 50·24″ *per annum*, the point of time denoted by our astronomical treatise is about 1672 years before 499 A.D., or about 1173 B.C. Archdeacon Pratt and Bentley, both of whom* had gone over the calculation, were of opinion that the observations indicated 1181 B. C.

The next question is to ascertain what it was that took place about 1173 B.C. of such consequence as to induce the ancient astronomers to record the astronomical positions for the event. Mr. R. C. Dutt states that 'tradition has it that when the Vedas were compiled the position of the solstitial points was observed and recorded to mark the date.' Professor Weber considers that both the Yajur Veda Samhitas may be shown from internal evidence to have assumed their present shape about the time of the war of the Mahabharata, and the Puranas relate that Vyasa, the compiler of the Vedas, lived about the time of the war. It is therefore proba-

*Max Muller's Rig Veda, Vol IV, Preface, p. XXVII.

ble that the astronomical positions refer to the period of the war which preceded the beginning of the Kaliyuga by a few years. The Jyotisha itself states that the first year of the 'Yuga' commenced at the winter solstice with the sun and the moon at the beginning of Dhanishta. In those early times there were two kinds of 'Yugas,' the five year cycle and the Kaliyuga.* It is hard to believe that the positions referred to in the Vedanga denote only the beginning of such a short-lived Yuga as the five year cycle. It is reasonable to suppose that they also mark the time of the commencement of the Kali with which probably began the first of a new series of five year cycles.

But it may be asked what authority there is, besides the Vedanga, to suppose that the Kali era began when the vernal equinox occurred with the sun in Bharani 10°. On the contrary, there might seem to exist sufficient evidence to suppose that at the time of the great war, which occurred a few years before the Kaliyuga began, the vernal equinox took place with the sun in the Krittikas. For example, there are many passages in the Taittiriya Samhita, the Taittiriya Brahmana and other Vedic

* Vedanga Jyotisha (Yajur Recension), verses 5–7. Aitareya Brahmana VII-15.

works where the Krittikas occupy the first place* in the list of the Nakshatras. The Krittikas are the mouth of Nakshatras, says the Taittiriya Brahmana (1. 1. 2. 1). In the Atharva Veda (1. 19. 7) and in the Yagnyavalkyasmriti, they occupy their early position, while the Vishnu Purana, as we have seen, actually places the vernal equinox in the beginning of the Krittikas. The Mahabharata says that the winter solstice took place sometime after the conclusion of the war on the fifth day after the new moon in the month of Magha,† and Hindu astronomers hold from such references that the vernal equinox was then in the Krittikas.‡ If therefore at the time of the war the equinox was in the Krittikas, it might appear that at the beginning of the Kali era, which very shortly followed the war, the vernal equinox could not have receded to Bharani 10°, that is, a precession of 3°.20′ which would take about 240 years to be accomplished. But this difficulty is easily explained.

It must be remembered that though the astronomical treatise gives only twenty-seven Nakshatras, the admittedly older works, the Atharva Samhita§

---

* See Max Muller's Rig Veda Vol. IV. Preface, p. xxxiv. Mr. Tilak's Orion, p. 39. *etseq.*

† Anusasana Parva, ch. 167. 26 and 27.

‡ Mr. Tilak's Orion, p. 37. footnote.

§ XIX. 7. 1. 81.

and the Taittiriya Brahmana* enumerate twenty-eight Nakshatras. What is more important is the fact that the list of the Atharva Veda connects the twenty-eight Nakshatras with as many days and that the lists of the Taittiriya Brahmana show the connection of these twenty-eight asterisms with a lunar synodical month. We may therefore infer that at the time of the compilation of these two Vedic works, the number of lunar asterisms was twenty-eight. But curiously enough we meet with only twenty-seven Nakshatras in the Taittiriya Samhita, where Abhijit is left out. So also the mention of 'trinava', twenty-seven, in the Taittiriya Samhita (VII. 1. 3. 2) refers probably to the twenty-seven Nakshatras. While on the one hand the Taittiriya Samhita is the oldest of these three nearly contemporaneous compilations, the list of the Taittiriya Brahmana is, on the other hand, mentioned in connection with an old kind of sacrifice called Nakshatreshti, a ceremony based on the supposition that there were twenty-eight Nakshatras. If we may judge by the generally received opinion that whatever is used for sacrificial purposes has the flavour of antiquity in it, possibly the original number was twenty-eight; and the mention of only twenty-seven Nakshatras in the Taittiriya Samhita†

* III. 1. 2. 5., III. 1, 5. 6.

† IV. 4. 10.

may be due to the fact that it was compiled under the immediate direction of the learned son (Vyasa) of a great astronomer (Parasara), the reputed author of an ancient astronomical treatise, who might have been the first to omit Abhijit from the list of the Nakshatras in order to suit his astronomical calculations. Professor Whitney and M. Biot hold that the original number was twenty-eight, while Professor Max Muller thinks that the number of Nakshatras was originally twenty-seven.* For our present purpose, it is enough to note that at the beginning of the Kaliyuga, when the compilation of the Taittiriya Samhita, at least in its original form, was completed and that of the Brahmana was almost begun, people were acquainted with both the lists. But from that time forward astronomers continued consistently to use twenty-seven Nakshatras only. From the earliest astronomical treatise known to us, namely, the Jyotisha Vedanga, to the latest work on Hindu astronomy, we find that all the Hindu astronomers, Garga, Aryabhata, Varahamihira, Brahmagupta, Bhascaracharya and many others regulate their calculations by the twenty-seven Nakshatra system. It is this number that is referred to in the Mahabharata,

* Rig Veda Vol. IV, Preface, p. xlvi.

Manu Smriti and the Vishnu Purana. We may therefore be sure that the number of twenty-eight Nakshatras which prevailed about the time of the compilation of the Atharva Veda Samhita and of the Taittiriya Brahmana was not adopted by later astronomers who preferred to use the more astronomically suitable number of twenty-seven Nakshatras.

The astronomers effected another improvement on the old method. The Nakshatras were made to begin with Dhanishta instead of with the Krittikas as of old. Somakara quotes an old saying of Garga in his commentary on the Vedanga Jyotisha (verse 5), तेषां च सर्वेषां नक्षत्राणां कर्मसु कृत्तिकाः प्रथममाचक्षते श्रविष्ठातु संख्यायाः ।, which means that "of these Nakshatras, the Krittikas are the first for sacrificial purposes and the Sravishta (Dhanishta) are the first for purposes of calculation." It is clear therefore that, in those early times referred to by Garga, the twenty-seven Nakshatras were counted from Dhanishta in works on astronomy. If the winter solstice was in the beginning of Dhanishta according to the Vedanga Jyotisha, the vernal equinox would be placed by astronomers in the end of the third quarter of Bharani. On the other hand, according to the twenty-eight Nakshatra system, if the winter solstice be at the same place, *i.e.*, in the beginning of Dhanishta, the vernal equinox will occur with the sun in the beginning of the Krittikas. The same point in the heavens, which, according to the twenty-seven Nakshatra system, denoted the end of the third *pada* of Bharani, also indicated the beginning of the Krittikas according to the twenty-eight Nakshatra system. It is therefore wrong to suppose, as scholars* have hitherto done, that the beginning of the Krittikas, mentioned in the Vedic works, denoted a point 3°20′ removed from the end of the third quarter of Bharani, mentioned by the Vedanga as the position for the vernal equinox. Thus the positions given in the Vedanga are the same as those indicated in the Vedic works, noticed at the time of the war and recorded in the Vishnu Purana. The Vedanga Jyotisha itself confirms this inference as in enumerating the deities presiding over the various Nakshatras it begins the list with Agni, the deity of the Krittikas, and not with Yama, the presiding Devata of the Bharani Nakshatra.

There is still another difficulty to encounter. It may be asked with reason how at such early times such an imaginary point in the heavens as the end of the third quarter of Bharani, without any star

* Mr. Tilak's Orion, p. 215.

to denote the position, could have been supposed to mark the vernal equinox. To answer this question this part of the heavens must be clearly laid before the mind's eye. Mrigasiras or the head stars of Orion are the earliest recorded beginners of the year, for with the sun near them the vernal equinox began the year in the very earliest period of Aryan history.* According to the Surya Siddhanta† the distance between the asterisms Mrigasiras and Rohini (Aldebaran) is stated to be 13°. 30′. The distances between Rohini and the Krittikas and between the latter and Bharani are stated to be 12° and 17°. 30′ respectively. As in those early times the heavens were divided into Nakshatras and Nakshatrapadas, and not into degrees and minutes, it must have been then crudely supposed that the distances between Mrigasiras and Rohini and between Rohini and the Krittikas represented nearly the arc covered by a divisional Nakshatra (*i. e.* 13°. 20′), that the distance between the Krittikas and Bharani denoted a divisional Nakshatra and that the distance between the Krittikas and Bharani denoted a divisional Nakshatra and a quarter. The divisional Mrigasiras would therefore begin with the asterism Rohini (Aldebaran) and the divi-

* Mr. Tilak's Orion, Chapters IV, V, VI and VII.

† Chapter VIII.

sional Rohini with the asterism Krittikas (Pleiades). The end of the divisional Krittikas would consequently coincide with the asterism Pleiades and its beginning would be placed about a *pada* after the asterism Bharani. Thus the position given by the Vedanga Jyotisha for the vernal equinox, namely, the end of the third *pada* of Bharani, was sufficiently identified as being distant from the stars Krittikas by one divisional Nakshatra and from the Stars Bharani by one Nakshatrapada.

We may therefore conclude that, at the beginning of the Kaliyuga, the vernal equinox took place with the sun at the end of the third *pada* of Bharani. As it is recorded that in 499 A. D. the vernal equinox occurred with the sun in the first point of Aswina, there was a precession of 23°. 20′ from the beginning of the Kali to 499 A.D.; that is, in other words, the Kali era began about 1173 B. C. It consequently follows that it is unreasonable to suppose, as some scholars have done, that the war happened about 1426 B. C. on the ground that the vernal equinox then took place with the sun in the Krittikas.

Secondly: The great Indian astronomer, Gargacharya, says in his Siddhanta when speaking of Salisuka, the fourth in succession from Asoka: "Then the viciously valiant Greeks, after reducing Saketa, Panchala country to Mathura, will reach Kusumadhwaja (Patna) : Pushpapura being taken, all provinces will undoubtedly be in disorder. The unconquerable Yavanas will not remain in the middle country. There will be cruel and dreadful war among themselves. Then after the destruction of the Greeks at the end of the Yuga, seven powerful kings will reign in Oudh." Mr. R. C. Dutt, from whose excellent work on Civilization in Ancient India the above translation is taken, remarks " we are then told that after the Greeks the rapacious Sakas were the most powerful and we have little difficulty in recognising in them the Yueti conquerors." The annals of Garga here come to an end. The very same foreign invasion is mentioned by Patanjali in his famous Mahabhashya on Panini. In commenting on the rule of Panini that the imperfect tense has to be used when the speaker refers to a past action, or (as Vararuchi adds in his Vartika) when the event related is out of sight but actually taking place at the same time, Patanjali illustrates the rule with the examples, "Arunadyavanah saketam," "Arunadyavano madhyamikan," " the Yavana besieged Saketa," " the Yavana besieged the Madhyamikas." The commentators on the Mahabhashya explain that Patanjali lived at the time, although not on the spot, when the Yavana besieged Oudh and the Madhyamikas. He refers also to " Mouryas," "Hall of

Chandragupta," and "Hall of Pushyamitra." From these references Dr. Goldstucker* infers that Patanjali lived about 144 B. C. But he was led to give that date because he thought that the Yavana invasion of Saketa and of the Madhyamikas referred to the Bactrian king Menander's invasion of Hindustan and encounter with the Buddhist Madhyamikas, the followers of Nagarjuna. Dr. Bhandarkar† infers that Patanjali wrote this particular portion about 144-142 B.C. on the ground that Menander is therein referred to and also for the reason that Patanjali speaks at the same place of sacrifices as still being performed for Pushpamitra.

It will be readily conceded that the word "Madhyamikas" denotes, as its etymology shows, the residents of the middle country, the same people that are referred to by Garga as the residents of the Madhyadesa or middle country. Patanjali himself explains the term to mean 'people or towns belonging to Madhyadesa'‡ and the Manusmriti § defines Madhyadesa to be the tract of country lying between the Himalayas in the north and the Vindhyas in the south and between Alla-

* Panini, p. 234.

† Indian Antiquary, I. 299 ; II. 59.

‡ Mahabhashya V.3.2.

§ Manusmriti II. 21.

habad in the east and Vinasana in the west. Consequently king Milinda's encounter with Nagarjuna and the Madhyamika sect recorded in Buddhistic legends need not be identified with the Yavana invasion referred to by Patanjali and Garga. Moreover Dr. Rajendralala Mitra* has shown that Menander never came as far as Oudh but only proceeded up to the Jumna, and in order that he might reach Oudh, he should have gone three hundred miles more to the eastward. That Garga does not refer to the invasion of Menander, which took place about 144 B. C., but to an earlier invasion of the Bactrian Greeks is proved by his referring it to the time of Salisuka who, according to the Vayu Purana, reigned for seven years after having ascended the throne 111 years from the date of Chandragupta or in the year 204 B. C.

In Madame Duff's recently published Chronology † of India, we find the following recorded :—

(1) 206 B. C. Antiokhos III of Syria, after making war on Euthydemos of Bactria, came to India and made a treaty with Sophagasenas (Subhagasena).

(2) 195 B. C. Demetrias of Bactria invades and reduces the Punjab.

* Indo - Aryans, Vol. II. p. 193.
† pp. 13 - 15.

(3) 181 B. C. Eukratides ruled in India as well as over Bactria. Mithridates I, seized some of his provinces.

(4) 180 B. C. The reigns of Euthydemos II., Antimakhos I, and of Pantaleon and Agathocles. The coins of the last two are still found in the Kabul valley, western Punjab and Kandahar.

(5) 165 B. C. The great Yueh-ti established themselves in Sogdiana by the expulsion of the Saka tribe, which thus dispossessed invaded Bactria.

(6) 144 B. C. Lassen places Menander about this date.

(7) 126 B. C. Bactria lost to the Saka tribe and wrested from it by the Yueh-ti.

It is clear from this list of dates, which confirms the statements of Garga in a marked manner, that between 206 B. C. and 165 B. C. many Bactrian kings reigned over the north-western borders of India, and some of them extended their conquests into the heart of northern Hindustan. These Bactrian chiefs seem to have often quarrelled among themselves until at last the Saka tribe, driven from their original homes by the Yueh-ti conquerors, in their turn attacked and defeated the Bactrians about 165 B. C. and established themselves in Bactria. The Bactrians were the Yavanas of Patanjali and Garga, as they were Greeks who were often styled as Yavanas by the Hindus. The statement of Garga that "there would be dreadful war among themselves and that in the end the Sakas would displace them" is justified by the many little wars among these Bactrians themselves who at last were sent away from Bactria by the Sakas. Mr. R. C. Dutt identifies these Sakas with the Yueh-ti conquerors; but this supposition is unnecessary, if not incorrect, because before the Yueh-ti conquerors came to Bactria, the Sakas were there in power. Garga, it has to be remembered, refers to the Sakas and not to the Yueh-ti. It would appear that when the Bactrians were confronted by the Sakas about 165 B. C. in Bactria, they retired from their Indian provinces in order to meet their new foes who threatened their very hearths and homes. As soon as the Yavanas retired, seven powerful kings are said to have reigned in Saketa or Kosala which, as we know from the Vishnu Purana and the Bhagavatha, was divided into seven parts or 'sapta kosalas.'

The Yavana invasion referred to by Patanjali and Garga occurred therefore a few years before

165 B. C., about which year, however, they retired from their Indian provinces. According to the Puranas, Pushyamitra subverted the Mauryan dynasty and began to reign in northern India 137 years after the accession of Chandragupta to the throne, *i.e.*, in 178 B.C. He is the father of the hero of Kalidasa's Malavikagnimitra, who according to the drama " defeated the Yavanas on the southern banks of the Indus." Probably this defeat also contributed to the retirement of the Greeks from the Madhyadesa. Kalidasa represents Pushyamitra as having been engaged in a great sacrifice when the victory over the Yavanas was gained and Patanjali states that sacrifices were being celebrated by Pushyamitra in his time. Moreover Patanjali refers to the Gargas so often as to induce Professor Weber to state that " the Gargas must have played a very important part at the time of the Mahabhashya, in the eyes of the author at all events."* It may also be noted that Garga's annals, which refer the beginning of the Yavana invasion to the time of Salisuka (204—197 B.C.), close rather abruptly with the narration of the destruction of these Yavanas. This fact shows that he could not have lived much later. For all the reasons above set forth, we may

* Indian Literature, p. 252.

conclude that Pushyamitra, Patanjali and Garga were almost contemporaries and lived about 165 B. C., the date of the retirement of the Bactrian Greeks from India. We may also suppose that Patanjali and Garga lived sometime before the invasion of Menander in 144 B.C., inasmuch as neither of them refers to the great Bactrian conqueror who overran Northern India and was of such consequence and renown as not only to find an honoured place in Buddhistic legends but also, according to Plutarch, to give rise, when he was no more, to a contention among several towns for the custody of his imperial ashes. That Garga lived about 165 B. C. is confirmed by a *Sloka* of his,* quoted by Bhattotpala in his commentary on Brihat Samhita, which means that if the sun were to turn to the north without reaching Dhanishta, it foretold great calamity. Garga is most probably referring in this prophetic strain to the conquest of the Yavanas which was such a calamitous occurrence. As the sun commenced to turn to the north without reaching Dhanishta about the year 216 B. C., when the winter solstice began to occur with the sun in Sravana, he must have lived only a little later when the change began to be felt. For if he had lived long after

* Mr. Tilak's Orion, p. 19.

this astronomical variation, he would not have noted it and regarded with any anxiety.

This retirement of the Yavanas is said by Garga to have occurred " at the end of the Yuga." What is the Yuga that he speaks of ? I am sure that it refers not to the shortlived five year cycle but to the other Yuga then in existence, the Kali Yuga. Garga himself speaks of the four Yugas, Krita, Treta, Dwapara and Kali, the third ending, and the fourth beginning, with the Mahabharata war. It will be shown, when the subject of the Yugas comes to be dealt with, that the Kali period was originally believed to consist of a thousand years. As the retirement of the Yavanas from India took place about 165 B. C., the Kali Yuga which ended about this time must have begun about 1165 B. C.

Thirdly: Megasthenes, the ambassador of Seleucus at the court of Chandragupta, has recorded in his writings the impressions he received while in India. His writings are known to us only in fragments from the works of Arrian, Pliny, Solinus, and others. Arrian (146 A.D.) quotes the following from Megasthenes: * "From the time of Dionysus to Sandracottus, the Indians counted 153 kings and a period of 6042 years; but among these a republic

* Mc Crindle's Ancient India pp. 203 and 204.

was thrice established, * and another to 300 years and another to 120 years." Pliny (41 A. D.), in quoting Megasthenes on the ancient history of the Indians, says: "For the Indians stand almost alone among the nations in never having migrated from their own country. From the days of Father Bacchus to Alexander the Great, their kings are reckoned at 154, whose reigns extend over 6451 years and 3 months."* Solinus (238 A. D.) is reported as stating:—"Father Bacchus was the first who invaded India and was the first of all who triumphed over the vanquished Indians. From him to Alexander the Great, 6451 years are reckoned with 3 months additional, the calculation being made by counting the kings who reigned in the intermediate period to the number of 153." † Thus there are three independent sources from which we can obtain an insight into the ancient chronology of India as known to the Greeks. It has to be noted that the legend of Dionysus or Bacchus and his connection with India is one of the most famous in Hellenic antiquity. Persecuted by the jealous Hera, Dionysus was exposed on Mount Nysa in Thrace from which he took his name (Dionysus = Nysa

*Hist. Nat. VI. XXI. 4, 5. Macrindle's Ancient India, p. 115.

† Mc Crindle's Ancient India, p. 115.

Sprung). In his long travels he is said to have reached India once upon a time, where he spent a few years in subduing its fierce tribes and teaching them, for so the story goes, the elements of cultivation, the pleasures of the grape, and the arts of civilization. In his *Anabasis*, the historian Arrian introduces the name of Dionysus in connection with another Nysa a city near the modern Cabul, which in about 327 B.C. surrendered to Alexander the Great. The troops of the Macedonian conqueror recognising in that city the limit of the conquests of Dionysus praised their leader as having surpassed even Dionysus in the extent of his conquests. Having found in Nysa near Cabul a verbal resemblance to the town of Nysa in Thrace, they naturally supposed that Dionysus must have gone so far east as India, and in this supposition they were confirmed by their tradition. Thus we can understand how the Greeks, always bent on identifying their legendary heroes with those of other countries, came to identify Bacchus (Dionysus) with Ikshvaku, the son of Vaivaswata Manu, who, according to Indian tradition, was the first to establish government and the arts of peace in Aryavarta. The Puranas give almost the same number of reigns from the time of Vaivasvata to the time of Chandragupta or Alexander. The number of kings given by these foreign historians "is eminently satisfactory as it seems clear that we possess in the Puranas the same lists as were submitted to the Greeks in the fourth century B. C. In the solar lists we have in the Treta Yuga 62 reigns from Ikshvaku to Rama. For the Dwapara age we have three solar lists: one from Kusha to Brihadbala, 35 reigns; another from Dishta to Janamejaya, 33 reigns; a third from the son of Siradhwaja, the father of Sita, to Mahabasi, 34 reigns. In the Kali Yuga we have no complete solar list, but the lunar list gives fifty descents from Jarasandha to the last Nanda. This gives 145 or 146 reigns.' * But with regard to the periods given in the three classical accounts, they have hitherto yielded nothing of historical value. Fergusson was of opinion that this part of the statement must be rejected as it gave an average duration of nearly forty years for each reign. "But," says he, "it is satisfactory to find that at that early age, the falsification of the chronology had only gone to the extent of duplication and that the monstrous system of Yugas, with their attendant absurdities had not then been invented.' But this is an unsatisfactory method of explaining the figures mentioned by the generally accurate classical historians. When the number of the kings

* Fergusson's History of Indian and Eastern Architecture, p. 712.

given by them tallies with that given by the Puranas, it may be asked how the number of years alone comes to be exaggerated. I believe that, far from being totally inaccurate, the years serve but to confirm the date fixed for the beginning of the Kali Yuga.

It has to be noted that the number of years given by so accurate a historian as Arrian differs from that given by Pliny who lived about a century earlier, and by Solinus who wrote about a century later, than Arrian. It has also to be remembered that every one of these scholars seems to quote from a common source, the writings of Megasthenes. But for the unfortunate destruction of the great Alexandrian library and the misguided vanity of the monks of early Christianity, who erased many valuable writings on the ancient papyrus rolls so as to give room for their own productions, we might have been overwhelmed with a wealth of ancient lore and tradition to illuminate many a dark problem relating to antiquity. Thus has been lost to the world the 'Indika' of Megasthenes and we are therefore to be content with the fragments quoted above from the other authors. Arrian states that 6042 years elapsed from the time of Ikshvaku to that of Chandragupta and that "among these" there were republics established for a period of about 420 years. We may suppose that the total for the reigns of the kings and for the republics comes to about 6042 + 420 or 6462 years,* a figure which very nearly approaches that given by the other two historians, 6451 years and 3 months. But inasmuch as we have for the latter figure the authority of two authors, one of whom was earlier by a century than Arrian, and inasmuch as both these writers are so exact as to give the number of months also in addition to the years elapsed, whereas Arrian deals vaguely in round figures in speaking of the republics, we ought to be satisfied that Megasthenes, the authority for all the three historians, must have stated that from the time of Ikshwaku to that of Alexander there had elapsed a period of 6451 years and 3 months. It is a matter of common knowledge that Alexander fought with Porus in the year 326 B. C., and left India for good in the year 325 B. C.†

To explain the number of years given by these historians, we shall have to advert to the Saptarshi

* As Pliny and Solinus give 6451 years for the interval between Ikshwaku and Alexander, and as Arrian gives 6462 years for the interval between Ikshwaku and Sandracottus, the two statements may perhaps be reconciled by our supposing that Chandragupta (315 B. C.) began to reign about 11 years later than Alexander's conquest of India (326 B. C.)

† M. Duff's Chronology of India, pp. 8 and 9.

cycle. We cannot at this distance of time explain satisfactorily what exactly our ancients had in mind when they laid down the mysterious proposition that the seven Rishis or the seven stars of Ursa Major moved on from Nakshatra to Nakshatra at the rate of one Nakshatra for every one hundred years. Bentley* supposed it to be a crude way of expressing what to the ancients was the inexplicable precession of the equinoxes. This imaginary motion is thus explained in the Vishnu Purana:—"When the two first stars (Pulaha and Kratu) of the seven Rishis (the Great Bear) rise in the heavens and some lunar asterism is seen at night at an equal distance between them, then the seven Rishis continue stationary in that conjunction for a hundred years of men. At the birth of Parikshit they were in Magha and the Kaliyuga, which consists of 1200 years, then commenced." † The commentator on the Bhagavata Purana says: "The two stars Pulaha and Kratu must rise or be visible before the rest; and whichever asterism is in a line south from the middle of these stars is that with which the seven stars are united and so they continue for one hundred years." Very much the same explanation is given

* Historical View of Hindu Astronomy, p. 65.

† Vishnu Purana, IV. 24.

by the Vayu and the Matsya Puranas.* Despite the authority of the venerable compilers of these Puranas, I am led to think that this explanation appears to be fantastic and opposed to astronomical science. It is true that the shifting of the equinoxes consequent on their precession may change the aspect of the starry sky with reference to the celestial poles. But as a matter of fact, the constellation of Ursa Major, which is stationed between the Leonis and the north pole of the heavens, cannot move on from Nakshatra to Nakshatra in the manner supposed by the Pauranikas. Indeed we are informed by the Puranas and the astronomers, Garga and Varahamihira, † that the Ursa Major was in [*i.e.*, was between the north pole and] the Magha Nakshatra (the Sickle) in the days of Yudhishtira; and as we find it even now to be located nearly in the same position, we may infer that the movement, far from being actual, was merely a convenient method to denote the march of time from the famous epoch of the Pandava Yudhishtira. Thus, if a certain event is stated to have occurred with the Saptarshis, say, in the Visakha Nakshatra, the statement does not signify that the Rishis have actually moved on to Visakha, but only

* Wilson's Vishnu Purana, Vol. IV. 233.

† Brihat Samhita XIII. 2 and 3.

means that the event took place in the sixth century after the epoch of Yudhishtira, Visakha being the sixth Nakshatra from Magha.

We have already seen that the number of Nakshatras popularly in use about the time of the compilation of the Atharva Veda Samhita and Taittiriya Brahmana was twenty-eight, including Abhijit, which Nakshatra was however left out by the Vedanga Jyotisha for enabling it to deal with astronomical phenomena in a scientific manner. But the change from twenty-eight to twenty-seven Nakshatras was confined for a long time to astronomers only. As the moon takes about 27¼ * days to make one complete circuit of the earth, the astronomers seem to have preferred the number of 27 Nakshatras, or "milestones of the heavens," as they have been appropriately termed, in order to make the moon's progress through each Nakshatra correspond to a civil day as nearly as possible. But for ordinary purposes the number of 28 Nakshatras seems to have been retained, as for instance, in the performance of Nakshatreshti sacrifices. As about the time of Yudhishtira the two Vedic works which refer to the twenty-eight Nakshatras were compiled, the cycle of the Saptarshis, which began with the epoch of Yudhishtira, appears to have

* 27 days, 7 hours, 46 minutes, and 12 seconds.

been originally a cycle of twenty-eight centuries. It is true that in Kashmir, where the Saptarshi cycle is even now prevalent, it is considered to be a cycle of twenty-seven centuries. This belief, however, is due to the fact that the twenty-seven Nakshatra system has become firmly established in India since the time of Aryabhata and Varahamihira. But at the time we are speaking of, namely, the reign of Chandragupta, the old popular way of counting twenty-eight Nakshatras was much in vogue and the Saptarshikala was therefore a cycle of 2800 years.

It is apparent from the Puranas that the different dynasties date from the beginning of the Treta Yuga and that Ikshwaku and Budha flourished at the beginning of the same Yuga. * The Puranas relate nothing of historicul interest as having taken place in the first or Krita age which is mainly occupied with the first four non-historic † Avatars of Vishnu. The Bhagavata ‡ says that Pururavas, the first king of the lunar line and the nephew of the first king of the solar line lived at the beginning of the Treta Yuga.

---

*Warren's Kala Sankalita, pp. 358 and 366. Fergusson's History of Indian and Eastern Architecture, p. 712. Bhagavata IX. 14.

† W. J. Wilkins' Hindu Mythology, p. 130.

‡ IX. 14. 49.

In the Uttarakanda of Valmiki Ramayana it is related that the Kshatriyas were born in the Treta Yuga.* It is therefore clear that both the solar and the lunar dynasties were supposed to have come into being in the beginning of the Treta Yuga, that is, two Yugas before the commencement of the Kali Yuga. In a subsequent chapter it will be shown, chiefly from references in the Rig Veda, that in Vedic times there existed a cycle of a thousand years, probably called 'Saptarshi Chakra', connected with the constellation of the Saptarshis, that there had intervened two such cycles between the time of Ikshwaku and that of Yudhishtira, that these two cycles were afterwards converted into the Treta and Dwapara Yugas of later chronology, and lastly that this Saptarshichakra was the direct parent of our Saptarshi cycle of twenty-eight centuries. The informants of Megasthenes, who were aware that two Saptarshichakras or cycles had preceded the war, naturally, though erroneously, supposed that two periods of 2,800 years each, or 5,600 years in all, had expired by that epoch. That the Saptarshi cycle was the guiding system of chronology about the time of Chandragupta is proved by a verse† of Garga

* Ch. 74.

† Brihat Sambita, XIII. 2 and 3.
See also Vishnu Purana IV. 24., where the age of Nanda is fixed in a similar manner.

which uses the Saptarshi periods to fix the date of the Saka (*sic*) kala. As Megasthenes gives 6451 years for the period between Ikshwaku and Alexander the Great and as 5,600 years were supposed to have expired at the beginning of the Kali Yuga, 6451–5600 or a duration of 851 years must have been the period represented to Megasthenes as having expired since the commencement of the new era. Since Alexander left India in 325 B. C., the Kaliyuga must have commenced, according to the informants of Megasthenes, in the year 851 + 325 or 1176 B. C.

There are five important erâs at present in use among Hindus in India of which the Vikrama and the Salivahana are the latest. The Saptarshi era is even now prevalent in Kashmir and the Kali is used generally in the rest of India. But the Malabar country is also guided by another era, called after Parasurama, which is also known as the Quilon or Kollam era. According to approved tradition it is a cycle of a thousand years and the present cycle, believed to be the fourth, began in the year 1825 A. D. But curiously enough, Mr. Logan thinks it to be an era beginning in 825 A. D., because no doubt that supposition suited his theory regarding the date of Cheruman Perumal, the supposed royal convert to Islam. Many scholars, like Drs. Caldwell, Gundert and Burnell, have tried to explain the true origin of the Kollam Andu, but their explanations do not seem to be satisfactory. The late Mr. P. Sundram Pillai discussed these opinions in a paper contributed to the *Madras Christian College Magazine* (Feb. 1897), and finding them unsatisfactory, suggested that the Kollam Andu was "a modification of another older era current in Upper India under the name of Saptarshaya or Sastra Samvatsara. The peculiarity of this northern era is that though it is to-day 4972, it is spoken of as 72, so that omitting the hundreds it would be found to be identical with our Malabar year except for four months beginning with Mesha." The Saptarshi begins with the month of Mesha; but the Kollam begins with Kanya in the north, and with Simha in the south, of Malabar. Mr. Sundram Pillai explains this divergence by supposing that in all probability the astronomers "found it necessary so to amend the northern luni-solar year in order to convert it into a purely solar one as the Kollam year professes to be." Mr. Sundram Pillai, however, ignores the fact of the Kollam Andu being a cycle and believes that it was adopted about 825 A.D. from the countries using the Saptarshi era. This is certainly a misconception and is due to the fact that the Kollam Andu at present counts also the thousand years of the last cycle in addition to the expired years of the present cycle. Thus the Kollam Andu for July 1901 is the 76th year of the fourth cycle; but it is now written as 1076 of the Kollam era. On the contrary, Lieutenant Col. Warren, who wrote his work, the learned Kalasankalita, just about the beginning of the present cycle in 1824 A. D., says of this Andu, "that there had expired on the 14th September, 1800, two cycles of a thousand years each and 976* years of the third cycle". Mr. R. Sewell states in his Indian Calendar † that the years of the Kollam Andu "run in cycles of thousand years. The present cycle is said to be the fourth. If there were really two cycles, ending with the year 1000, which expired 824-5 A. D., then it would follow that the Kollam era began in Kali 1927 current or the year 3528 of the Julian period." Warren relied on a still earlier authority, Dr. Buchanan, who stated "that the inhabitants of Malayala reckoned time in cycles of thousand years from 1176 B.C. and that in September 1800 A.D., there were two cycles and 976 years expired of that era."‡ We have therefore the authority of three eminent writers, two of whom lived before the commencement of the present cycle, to the

* Must be 975 years. Kalasankalita, p. 374. See Sewell's Indian Calendar, p. 45, footnote.

† P 45.

‡ Must be 975 years. Kalasankalita, p. 298.

effect that the Kollam era is really a thousand year cycle beginning in August or September 1176 B. C.

Not only is the Kollam Andu a cycle of a thousand years but it is also identical with the old Saptarshi cycle which is referred to by Albiruni (1030 A.D.), Kalhana (1148 A. D.) and the Puranas. As many manuscripts in the Deccan College are said to be dated in the Saptarshi era, this era seems to have once been much more widely used than at present. Though the Kashmirians now state that this era began in 3076 * B. C., it will be shown in a later chapter that about the time when the chronological portion of the Vishnu Purana was reduced to its present form, the Saptarshi era was supposed to begin a hundred years earlier, or in 3176 B. C., that the Vedic 'Saptarshichakra' cycle of a thousand years, the first cycle of which began in 3176 B. C. and the second cycle of which ended in 1176 B. C., was the direct parent of, and was immediately followed by, the modern Saptarshi kala. The Kollam Andu too is a cycle of a thousand years and began in 1176 B. C. Is it not then most likely that both the Saptarshi and Kollam cycles are almost identical? The earliest starting point for the modern Saptarshi kala is the

* R. Sewell's Indian Calendar, p. 41.

" birth of Parikshit when the Rishis were in Magha and the Kali Yuga then commenced." * Thus the Puranas identify the Saptarshi Kala with the Kali Yuga. As the Kollam era has been identified with the Saptarshi era, we may safely conclude that the Kollam Andu, the Saptarshi Kala, and the Kali Yuga, all commenced in 1176 B.C.

The Kollam era seems to have been brought into Malabar by the Aryan Namburi immigrants at some remote period in the annals of southern India. " Everything about the Namburi society is hoary with age," says Mr. V. Nagam Aiya in his report on the Census of Travancore. What has been altogether forgotten by the Hindus in the rest of India, Kashmir alone excepted, is still retained by these extremely conservative people of Malabar. But the very same reason which accounts for the disappearance of this era in the rest of India also contributed to the origin of the era being forgotten in Malabar. In the beginning of the sixth century A.D., the astronomers made the Kali Yuga begin in 3102 B.C., and the authority of Aryabhata and Varahamihira was supreme enough to cause the spread of the new doctrine throughout the length and breadth of India. The people of Malabar, who were led therefore to believe that the

* Vishnu Pŭrana, IV. 24.

Kali began in 3102 B.C., connected their era, which really began with the commencement of the Kali era in 1176 B.C., with the venerable name of Parasurama, the supposed leader of the Aryan immigration into Malabar.

It is strange that, to this day, it is a Namburi Brahman that is the ministering priest at the shrine of Kedarnath in the Himalayas and at Jagannath in Orissa. It is also curious that not only in chronology, but also in architecture, laws and usages, the northernmost parts of India have much in common with the Malabar country. Dr. Fergusson and Mr. J. D. Mayne are both struck by this remarkable coincidence. Whatever be the explanation for this resemblance, we may be perfectly sure that the extremely conservative tendency of Malabar has very largely helped to preserve it. Of all the peoples in India, the Malayalis, Brahmans and non-Brahmans alike, still preserve their respective old institutions with a pious heroic conservatism worthy of a better cause. If Western education has undermined this pathetic attachment to the old order of things, we can only hope that those to whom has been entrusted the shaping of their new destiny will consider the claims of the old in paving the way for the new.

CHAPTER II.

THE DATE OF THE MAHABHARATA WAR.

IN the last chapter it was attempted to fix the date of the beginning of the Kaliyuga from testimony derived from four different sources. From the data furnished by the astronomical work called Vedanga Jyotisha, it was inferred that the era must have begun about 1173 B. C. From the statement made by the astronomer Gargacharya, we drew the conclusion that it must have commenced a few years before 1165 B. C. On examining the figures given by the classical historians, we found that it began 851 years before the date of Alexander's stay in India, or in 1177—76 B. C., a date which, we saw, was confirmed by the evidence of the Malabar Kollam Andu which commenced in 'August or September,' 1176 B. C. As the Vedanga Jyotisha, which refers to the period of the commencement of the Kaliyuga, begins the year with the winter solstice,* we may well suppose that the Kaliyuga began with the winter solstice immediately prece-

* Yajur Vedanga Jyotisha: Verses 6 and 7.

ding the commencement of the Kollam Andu, or at the end of 1177 B. C. It is proposed in this chapter to examine fresh materials and to fix the date of the great Mahabharata war which was fought a few years before the beginning of the Kaliyuga.

It is unanimously declared in the Mahabharata* and in all the Puranas † that as long as Sri Krishna remained on earth, the Dwaparayuga continued and with his death commenced the Kali age. "As long as the earth was touched by His holy feet, the Kali age could not affect it. * * But the day that Krishna shall have departed from the earth will be the first of the Kaliyuga."‡ On hearing of his death, his devoted admirers, the Pandavas, did not care any longer to hold the reins of government, which indeed they would have already resigned, but that their grandson and heir, Parikshit, had until then been too young to be trusted with the cares of an empire. The sweets of the purple had, in fact, never § been acceptable to them, inasmuch as their victory was

* Mahaprasthanika parva, I, 2 and 7.

† Wilson's translation of Vishnu Purana, Vol. IV. p. 234.

‡ *Ibid.*

§ Santi Parva, VII, XXV, and LXXV.

bought at too dear a price and only after a terrific carnage of all their dearest friends and relatives in that tremendous war. The death of Sri Krishna proved to be the proverbial last straw and the Pandavas once for all determined to quit a world fraught with so many painful recollections. There is a pathetic fable current in Southern India that when Yudhishtira was ruling his empire with even-handed justice, he suddenly found on a certain day an unjust claim set up before him by a litigant who, only the day before, had been pleading the cause of righteousness. The virtuous monarch was astounded by this unprecedented and sudden decline in virtue and attributed it to the influence of the Kaliyuga, the dawn of which was then being expected. He forthwith resolved never more to witness the vices of the sinful age and, having established Parikshit in the sovereignty of his realm, departed with his brothers on his grand Mahaprasthana. Whatever may be the reason that ultimately induced the Pandavas to retire from their worldly duties, it is evident that they were enabled to carry out their resolve the more easily by the fact that Parikshit had just then arrived at age. It has to be remembered that in precocious India Hindu lawyers fix the age of majority in the sixteenth year. As Parikshit was born soon after the close of the war, the beginning of the Kali age, which is coeval with the coronation* of Parikshit, must be placed about sixteen years after the war; and if the Kali commenced in 1177 B. C., Parikshit must probably have been born in 1193 B. C. and the war should have taken place towards the end of the year 1194 B. C.

But the epic relates that the race of Sri Krishna was destroyed 36† years after the war and that the Pandavas left their kingdom soon after at the beginning of the Kaliyuga. The compiler of the epic, who wants us here to believe that the Kali commenced 36 years after the war, on another occasion‡ places the beginning of the Kali at the time of the war itself. It is not safe to rely on every statement contained in the epic, because it is neither the work of one author nor of one age.§

---

* Wilson's Vishnu Purana, Vol. IV. p. 232.

† Mausala Parva, I. 1 and 3.

‡ Bhagavatyana Parva, Sec. CXLII.

§ Telang's Introductions to Bhagavat Gita, Sanatsujatiya, and Anugita in the Sacred Books of the East Series, Vol. VIII; Wilson's Introduction to Vishnu Purana; Prof. Macdonell's Sanskrit Literature, p. 285. Weber's Indian Literature, pp. 187 and 188; Monier Williams's Indian Wisdom, XIII. p. 371.

We can find other statements in the epic nearly contradicting the statements above set forth. The Mahabharata states that after the expiry of fifteen years after the war, old Dhritarashtra left with his wife and Kunti for the forest glades to enable him to lead the holy life of a recluse. In the sixteenth year after the war, the Pandavas are said to have set out on a visit to these old people, taking with them all their male and female relatives. We are told that Uttara, the wife of Abhimanyu, "who had recently become a mother,"* was also among the number, "with her child (Parikshit) in her lap."† It must be borne in mind that Parikshit was conceived sometime before the war, as he was the son of Abhimanyu who had lost his life in the war. The Mahabharata expressly states that Parikshit was *in gremio matris* during the progress of the war.‡ Consequently he could not have been a baby at the breasts in the sixteenth year after the war. As this statement is therefore incorrect, I am disposed to believe that in the sixteenth year after the war the Pandavas started, not on a visit to these old people, but on their last journey, the Mahaprasthana. Moreover, one may be

* Asramavasika Parva, XV. 10.

† *Ibid.* XXV. 15.

‡ Sauptika Parva, XVI. 7 and 8.

struck by the fact that while much irrelevant and extraneous matter is crowded into the epic, the marriage of Parikshit alone is not mentioned. The reason evidently is that Parikshit was young and unmarried when the Pandavas rather suddenly handed over the kingdom to him on hearing of the death of that great hero-philosopher, that *alter ego* of Pandava Arjuna, Sri Krishna Vasudeva. The Mahabharata concludes with the narration of their last journey and 'ascent to heaven,' and most probably the marriage of Parikshit took place sometime later. Besides, if Parikshit were really 36 years of age at this time, how is it that Yudhishtira placed him at the time of their departure under the tutelage of Kripacharya?* It would be more consistent with the general drift of the epic if we hold that Parikshit was about sixteen years of age when he was placed in charge of the Kaurava Empire and that the Mahabharata war occurred about sixteen years before the beginning of the Kaliyuga. We shall presently find that there are other grounds which go to support such a conclusion.

The only indigenous work in all India that can pass for history is the Rajatarangini, the well-known history of Kashmir, written in 1148 A. D.

* Mausala Parva, VII. 14.

by Kalhana Pandit. It states* that the author put together the details deduced from his examination, not only of the *sasanas* of the previous kings recording the consecration of temples and grants to them, but also of the laudatory inscriptions and of *sastras* current in his time. Dr. Hultzsch and M. Troyer translate thus the verses 48 and 49 of the first Taranga:—'Misled by the tradition that the Bharata war took place at the end of the Dwapara(yuga), some have considered as wrong the sum of years (contained in the statement that,) in the Kaliyuga, the kings beginning with Gonanda I. (and ending with Andha Yudhishtira) ruled over the Kasmiras for 2268 years.'† This Gonanda I. was, according to the Rajatarangini,‡ the contemporary of the great Pandavas of the Mahabharata fame. The fifty-second in descent from Gonanda I. was Abhimanyu, the son of Kanishka, whose successor, Gonanda III., was the first of a new dynasty 'which came to power 2330 years before Kalhana's time.'§ But as we find in the Rajatarangini that the actuals for the reigns from the end of the reign of Andha Yudhishtira, the last of the dynasty of Gonanda III., to Kalhana's own time amount to 1329 years, 3 months and 28 days, or roughly

* First Taranga, Verse 15.

† Indian Antiquary, April 1889.

‡ I. 44. § I. 52 and 53.

1330 years, Kalhana must have supposed that the interval between the end of Abhimanyu's reign and that of Andha Yudhishtira's represented a period of (2330—1330, or) 1000 years. From the extract given above, it is clear that in Kalhana's time the belief was current that there had elapsed 2268 years from the time of Pandava Yudhishtira to that of Andha Yudhishtira. Consequently Kalhana gives(2268—1000,or)1268 years for the reigns of the first fifty-two kings from Gonanda I. to Abhimanyu. We are now in a position to understand what the 'tradition',* referred to by Kalhana actually was. It must have been supposed that 1268 years had elapsed from the time of the coronation of Pandava Yudhishtira, the contemporary of Gonanda I., to the time of Abhimanyu, and that the twenty-one kings of the dynasty of Gonanda III. reigned in all for one thousand years. We may go even further and infer that the original tradition was to the effect that 1268 years had elapsed from the time of the great war to the time of Kanishka's successor, and that the period of 1000 years, allotted to the twenty-one kings of the second dynasty, is a later addition, regard being had to the large average for each reign and the roundness of the figure. As

* I. 48 and 49.

a matter of fact, Kalhana himself actually states that it is "thought" that the fifty-two kings down to Abhimanyu reigned in all "for 1266* years."

But we may well be surprised with the actual dates given by the historian. As we may infer from the verses 48 and 49 of the first Taranga, he accepts the old tradition in so far as it stated that 2268 years had elapsed from the time of Pandava Yudhishtira to that of Andha Yudhishtira; but with regard to the other part of the tradition, namely, that Pandava Yudhishtira lived at the end of the Dwapara Yuga, Kalhana does not accept it. The reason for Kalhana's standpoint was that, in his day as now, the Dwapara was supposed to have ended, and the Kaliyuga to have begun, in 3102 B. C., whereas he placed greater reliance on a verse† of Garga, quoted in Varahamihira's Brihat Samhita, which he interpreted, erroneously as will shortly appear, as meaning that Yudhishtira commenced to reign 2526 years before the era of Salivahana, or in 2448 B. C. As Abhimanyu lived 1268 years after Pandava Yudhishtira, Kalhana therefore placed him in (2448—1268, or) 1180 B. C. Since Kanishka and his successor Abhimanyu lived in the first century after

* Evidently a mistake for 1268 years. I. 54.

† Brihat Samhita, XIII, 3 and 4.

Christ, it will be readily seen that the false figures given by Kalhana for Abhimanyu and all the subsequent kings down to the sixth century A. D. can be traced to his mistaken interpretation of the tradition and of the verse of Garga referred to by him.

The verse of Garga will be shortly discussed in another connection. But at present it is enough to concern ourselves with Kalhana's premises, and not with his dates. As we have seen, he proceeded on an ancient tradition that from the time of Yudhishtira to the time of Abhimanyu, the successor of Kanishka, there was an interval of 1268 years. Though the late General Cunningham thought that the Vikrama era dating from 57 B.C. began with Kanishka, yet almost all Sanskrit* scholars are now agreed that he lived in the first century after Christ and that probably the Saka era, which began on the 3rd of March 78 A. D., dates from this influential monarch. Without, however, entering into this vexed question, we may broadly state that Kanishka is proved by coins† to have reigned down to 40 A. D. Whether or not the era

* See M. Duff's Chronology of India, p. 21, where all the authorities are collected.

† Lassen in Indische Alterthumskunde, II, 413, quoted in Weber's Indian Literature, pp. 218 and 219,

of Salivahana dates from Kanishka, it is clear that Abhimanyu must have been reigning about the commencement of that era in 78 A. D. If so, Yudhishtira, who lived 1268 years earlier, must have begun to reign about(1268—78, or) 1190 B.C. As the* coronation of Yudhishtira took place soon after the close of the war, we may suppose that the Mahabharata war also was fought about the year 1190 B.C.

In the year 476 A. D. was born the greatest of Hindu astronomers, Aryabhata by name, whose fame spread not only in India and Arabia but also in the vast dominions of the Greek Empire of Constantinople. He was known to the Arabs under the name of Arjabahr and to the Romans as Andubarius or Ardubarius.† He was the first in India to promulgate the bold theory that it was the earth ‡that revolved round the sun. His calculation of ‡the circumference of the earth and his explanation of the phenomena of the eclipses‡ prove beyond doubt that he richly deserved all the encomiums showered upon him by Hindus and foreigners

* Santi Parva, XLI. 23.

† 'Chronicon Paschale,' quoted in Weber's Indian Literature, p. 255.

‡ Dutt's Ancient India, Vol. II. p. 243.

alike. He is reported to have stated* "that the line of the Saptarshis intersected the middle of Magha Nakshatra in the year of Kaliyuga 1910," *i.e.*, 1192 B.C. It has already been shown that the Puranas † relate that the Rishis were in the very same position at the birth of Parikshit. Combining the testimony of the Puranas with that of Aryabhata, we may readily infer that Parikshit was born about 1192 B.C. As the war took place at the most a few months earlier than the birth of Parikshit, it might have occurred about 1193 B.C.

We arrive at the very same result if we take into consideration the number of kings who, according to the Puranas, occupied the throne of Magadha from the time of the war to the accession of Chandragupta. The Vishnu Purana states what the other Puranas mainly agree in recording, namely, that the nine Nandas reigned for a hundred years, that the ten Saisunagas of the next previous dynasty reigned for 362 years, that the five kings of the still previous Pradyota dynasty occupied the throne for 138 years, and that this last dynasty succeeded the famous Barhadratha dynasty, twenty-two kings of which occupied the throne of Magadha since the date of the War. Thus we get 100

* Warren's Kala Sankalita, p. 380.

†See Wilson's Translation of Vishnu Purana, Vol IV, p. 33.

years for the Nandas and 500 years for the two previous dynasties. We have to bear in mind that it is unsafe to implicitly believe in everything that the Puranas relate. It is rather our duty to "prove all things and hold fast that which is good." The number of kings given by them is probably correct inasmuch as it is very probable that the same number was reported to the Greek Ambassador Megasthenes. But we have to pause before accepting the *periods*. At first sight one would remark the round figures for the periods allotted to these dynasties, namely, 100 years for the Nandas and 500 years for the Pradyotas and Saisunagas. What, however, strikes one most is the large average number of years for each reign. The very same Vishnu Purana gives 137 years for the ten kings of the later Maurya dynasty, 112 years for the ten kings of the Sunga dynasty, and 45 years for the four kings of the Kanwa line. The average number of years for each king of these post-Chandragupta dynasties is about 12 years. But the average for the Pradyota dynasty is about 28 years and that for the Saisunaga about 36 years! As for the Nandas, it is scarcely probable that a father and his sons could have reigned for one hundred years, especially when we remember that the last surviving son's did not die a natural death, but were extirpated by Chandragupta with the aid of the scheming Chanakya.* As the years given by the Purana for these pre-Chandragupta dynasties are therefore not trustworthy, it would be unsafe to deduce therefrom the probable date of the war. It is possible that the Puranas may have left out insignificant reigns, or that these ancient kings were more robust and long-lived than the kings of the post-Chandragupta period; but even on that supposition, the averages are still too large.

In hardy old England, from the Norman invasion to the beginning of the twentieth century, thirty-five monarchs had reigned, the commonwealth counting as one king, for a period of 835 years, and the average for each reign is about twenty-three years. From the accession of Hugh Capet of the House of Valois to the execution of Louis XVI, France † had been ruled over by thirty-three kings for a period of (1793–987, or) 806 years, yielding an average of about twenty-four years. Eight kings had ruled over Prussia † from the accession of Frederick I. to the death of Frederick II. in 1888 A. D., or for a period of 187 years with an average of about twenty-three years. In Russia,† from the time of Ivan III., there

* See Visakhadatta's Mudra-Rakshasa and Dhundiraja's Introduction thereto. Mahawanso, Ch. IV.

† George's Geneological Tables of Modern History.

had reigned twenty-two monarchs up to the accession of the present Emperor Nicholas II. for a period of (1894—1462, or) 432 years, which results in an average of about nineteen years. In old Japan, the present Emperor Mutsu Hito is supposed to be "the 123rd of the Imperial line, his ancestor Jimmu Tenno, the first Emperor, having established the dynasty which has lasted unbroken for 2500 years."* This gives about twenty-one years for each king of this long-lived dynasty. Thus we have the averages for each of the five foremost Powers of our Hemisphere, 23 years for England, 24 for France, 23 for Germany, 19 for Russia, and 21 for Japan. We may not be far wrong if we take the average of these averages, *i.e.* about 22 years, as the probable duration of each reign of the pre-Chandragupta dynasties. There were twenty-two Barhadrathas, five Pradyotas and ten Saisunagas, or thirty-seven kings in all, from the time of the War to that of the Nandas and they might therefore have reigned for about (37 × 22, or) 814 years. Moreover, according to the Bnddhistic 'Mahawanso,' composed by Mahanama at about 460 A. D., Mahapadma Nanda, called Kalasoko in the chronicle, reigned for twenty years and

* Rev. Herbert Moore's Half-hours in Japan, p. 250.

"had ten sons. These brothers conjointly ruled the empire righteously for 22 years. Subsequently there were nine brothers: they also according to seniority righteously reigned for 22 years."* That is to say, the Nandas reigned in all for a period of (20 + 22 + 22, or) 64 years, a figure more likely to be correct than the Puranic 100 years. Thus, according to our method of reckoning, the War must have happened about (814 + 64, or) 878 years before Chandragupta, or at about (878 + 315 †, or) 1193 B. C.

We have stated above that there was an interval of about 814 years between the War and the accession to the throne of Mahapadma Nanda. But the Vishnu Purana gives 1015‡ years for the period or about 200 years more than our figure. The compiler of the Purana appears to have arrived at 1015 years by supposing that a round period of 1000 years elapsed from the commencement of the Kaliyuga to the time of Nanda's accession and that the Kali began 15 years later than the war. If this surmise of ours be correct, we may well suspect the genuineness of the interval of a round period of a thousand years between the beginning of Kali and

* Turnour's Mahawanso, Ch. IV.

† Max Muller's Ancient Sanskrit Literature, p. 298.

‡ Vishnu Purana, IV. 24.

the coronation of Nanda. Moreover, the Purana period of 1015 years for the 37 kings between the War and the coronation of Nanda yields an improbable average of a little over 27 years. That the author deals vaguely in round figures is evident from his giving 100 years for the Nandas, 500 years for the Pradyotas and Saisunagas, and 1000 * years for the Barhadratha dynasty; and this last figure directly conflicts with the other statement that 1015 years intervened between the war and the end of the Saisunaga dynasty.

There is another statement in this Purana to the effect that the Saptarshis, which are supposed to move at the rate of one Nakshatra for every hundred years,† had moved ten Nakshatras from Magha to Purvashada during this interval, which therefore comes to (10 × 100, or) 1000 years. It will be apparent that this supposed movement was arrived at by the author, not by its having been previously actually observed and noted, for such a movement is astronomically impossible, but by his deducing it from his other statement, contained in the immediately preceding verse, that 1015 years had elapsed during this interval. In fact the author seem *first* to have had in mind that the Kali began 15 years

* Vishnu Purana, IV. 23.

† Vishnu Purana, IV. 24.

after the war and that 1000 years elapsed from the beginning of the Kali era to the accession of Nanda to the throne of Magadha, and *next* to have deduced therefrom the proposition that the Saptarshis, which were in Magha at the time of the war, had moved on to Purvashadha at the coronation of Mahapadma Nanda.

In chapter XIII of the Brihat Samhita, Varahamihira, who was born in 505 A. D., deals with the subject of the Saptarshi cycles. After premising that he quotes from Vriddha Garga, he states :—

आसन्मघासु मुनयः शासति पृथ्वीं युधिष्ठिरे नृपतौ ।
षड्द्विकपञ्चद्वियुतः शककाल स्तस्य राज्ञश्च ॥ ३ ॥

This sloka has been thus translated by Dr. Hultzsch * :— "When king Yudhishtira ruled the earth, the (seven) seers (Ursa Major) were in Magha; the Saka era (is) 2526 (years after the commencement) of his reign." He comments on it by saying: "Accordingly the coronation of Yudhishtira took place 2526 years before the commencement of the Saka era, or at the expiration of the Kaliyuga-Samvat 653 and in B. C. 2448." It may be observed that Dr. Hultzsch agrees with Kalhana in †

*Indian Antiquary, VIII, p. 66.

† Rajatarangini, I. 56.

thinking that the Yudhishtira era is different from the Kali era. On the other hand, Jyotirvidabharana, an astronomical work ascribed to Kalidasa, but which scholars place in the sixteenth century * A. D., tells us that in the Kaliyuga six different eras will flourish one after another; the Yudhishtira to last for 3044 years from the beginning of Kali, the Vikrama era to last for 135 years afterwards, the Salivahana for 18000 years after the Vikrama era, and the Vijaya, Nagarjuna, and Bali eras to be current in the rest of the Kaliyuga. Of course these three last eras are fictitious and have nothing to do with our enquiry. But I quote the Jyotirvidabharana only for the purpose of showing that Hindus have all along thought that the Yudhishtira era commenced with the Kali. So also Aryabhata computes by the era of Yudhishtira,† which corresponds to the Kaliyuga. It is not therefore possible to concur with Kalhana and Dr. Hultzsch who place the beginning of the Yudhishtira era "at the expiration of the Kaliyugasamvat 653 and in B. C. 2448."

We have to consider what the word 'Sakakala' really means. It has been already proved that

* Weber's Indian Literature, p. 201.

†Colebrooke's Mis: Essays, Vol. II, p. 428. Weber's Indian Literature, p. 260.

Garga, the author of the sloka, lived about 165 B. C. Even granting, for the sake of argument, the contention of Dr. Kern that Garga lived in the first century B. C., it is not possible that Garga could have meant by 'Sakakala' either the Vikramasamvat, which began rather subsequently in 57 B. C., or the Salivahana Sakabda, which commenced still later in 78 A. D. It may also be noted here that it has not been as yet proved that the Vikramasamvat era had been in use ever since 57 B. C. On the contrary, scholars like Fergusson,* Max Muller† and Weber‡ are of a different opinion. Besides the Kali or the Saptarshi era, there was in the days of Garga only one other prominent era in existence, namely, the era of Nirvana, "which," says Fergusson§ in connection with a different subject, "as far as I can see was the only one that had existed previously in India." The era of Mahavira, the founder of Jainism,

* History of Indian and Eastern Architecture, p.46; Fergusson's 'On the Saka, Samvat and Gupta Eras', pp. 11—16.

† India, what can it teach us. 1st edition, note G; and Preface to 2nd edition, p. XVII.

‡ Indian Literature, p. 202.

§ Fergusson's History of Indian and Eastern Architecture, p. 742.

beginning in 527 B. C., might have been then in existence; but the Jain religion was only confined comparatively to a few and its era was not much in evidence before the public. The era of Buddha's Nirvana was, on the other hand, very widely known both by reason of the intrinsic merits of His beautiful creed and of its constitution as the State Religion during the time of Asoka the Great. In a Tibetan work a schism * is recorded as having occurred under a 'Thera Nagasena' 137 years after the Nirvana; Chandragupta is recorded to have ascended the throne 162 years† after the Nirvana; the inauguration of Asoka is stated to have taken place 218 years † after the Nirvana; and the Dipawanso, a history of Ceylon written in Pali verse about the fourth century A.D., makes use of the era of Nirvana in its computations. Therefore the era of Buddha's Nirvana which was in current use in the time of Garga might have been probably referred to by him.

It is well-known that Gautama Buddha was known by the name of Sakya Muni and that his paternal grandfather was also known by the name of Sakya. Every reader of that noble classic, Sir Edwin Arnold's Light of Asia, is

* The Theosophist, Nov. 99, p. 109.

† Max Muller's Ancient Sanskrit Literature, p. 299.

aware that the race to which Gautama belonged was often called by the name of Sakyas, as for example, where king Suddhodana was asked by his minister to

> "Command a festival
> Where the realm's maids shall be competitors
> In youth and grace and sports that *Sakyas* use."

Says Mr. R. C. Dutt, "A little to the east of the Kosala kingdom, two kindred clans, the Sakyas and the Koliyans, lived on the opposite banks of the small stream Rohini. * * Kapilavastu was the capital of the Sakyas.*" The followers of Gautama Buddha were often spoken of as 'Sakyaputriya Sramanas', in contradistinction possibly to the Sramanas of other sects. We may therefore infer that the era of Gautama Buddha was probably known as 'Sakya Kala' in those times. The era could not have been called by the name of 'Nirvana Kala', for the evident reason that the term might equally apply to the Nirvana of Mahavira, the Jaina Saint.

The sloka quoted above is written in the usual Arya metre, whose nature is thus defined in works on Sanskrit rythm :—

यस्याः पादे प्रथमे द्वादशमात्रास्तथा तृतीयेपि ।
अष्टादश द्वितीये चतुर्थके पञ्चदश सार्या ॥

* Ancient India, Vol. I. p. 320.

which means: "The first and the third quarters must each contain twelve matras, or syllabic instants (one being allotted to a short vowel and two to a long one), the second eighteen and the fourth fifteen". The sloka next following the one in question is the fourth in the chapter and satisfies the conditions required. Similarly, the first two slokas of the chapter are in faultless rythm. But with regard to the third sloka, which is the one under discussion, only the first three quarters satisfy our rythmic requirements. The last quarter, शककालस्तस्य राज्ञश्च, is however short by one matra. It is inexplicable how scholars, including Kalhana, could have hitherto overlooked such a glaring slip. From the fact that the Rajatarangini also makes this mistake, we may infer that the error might have been in existence from a very long time. It strikes me that the only way of correcting the error is by the insertion of the letter '*y*,' which has been somehow omitted, between the letters '*k*' and '*a*' in the word 'Saka.' If the expression 'Sakakala' be corrected into 'Sakyakala,' or 'Sákyakala,' the sloka becomes perfect and we shall have then the best of reasons to suppose that Garga refers to the era of Nirvana. 'Sakyakala' or 'Sákyakala' would then denote the epoch of the Sakyas, or of the Sakya prince Gautama, or of the Buddha called Sakya Muni. Most probably some early copyist, better acquainted with Sakakala than with Sakyakala, changed the latter into the former which he might have thought to be the correcter form. Even without the aid of such a correction, 'Sakakala' may be considered to be a corruption of the word 'Sakyakala.' Thus in any case the era of Buddha's Nirvana is the one most undoubtedly referred to.

We have next to determine what is meant by the phrase षड्द्विकपञ्चद्वि. As we have seen, Dr. Hultzsch interprets it as meaning 2526. But if only we look into the expression a little closely, we may arrive at quite a different result. In the Sanskrit language it is usual, when numerical expressions are employed, to put the units first, the tens after the units, the hundreds after the tens and the thousands after the hundreds, and so on. Thus, for instance, the number one hundred and twenty-five is written thus: five two one. Dr. Hultzsch thinks that the expression now being discussed is written thus: Six two five two, which, expressed in English figures, denotes 2526. But we have to take note of the letter 'क' in the middle of the expression षड्द्विकपञ्चद्वि. द्विक means 'twice', 'two times', 'a collection of two,' but not 'two' simply. If 'क' were a mere expletive used for the purpose of metre, it may be asked why द्वय, which means 'two' simply, has not been used in preference to the ambiguous द्विक. When affixed to numerals the termination क is not an expletive and generally denotes 'so many times.' Such a precise mathematician like Garga cannot be expected to use the particle unnecessarily, especially when quite a different meaning is thereby rendered possible. In my opinion, the word षड्द्विक means 'twenty-six times,' and पञ्चद्वि means 'twenty-five'; in other words, the whole expression signifies "twenty-six times twenty-five," or 650.

If it be asked why such a round-about method of expression has been adopted to denote the simple number of 650 years, it may be urged in reply that Garga professedly computed here by the Saptarshī cycle which denoted the lapse of every one hundred years by a new Nakshatra, and gave twenty-five years for each Nakshatrapada, into four of which a Nakshatra was then, as we have already seen, usually divided. If the Rishis had moved 6½ Nakshatras from the time of the coronation of Yudhishtira to the Nirvana of Buddha, that would be more appropriately expressed as the movement of the Rishis through twenty-six padas and the period denoted thereby would be put down as twenty-six times twenty-five years.

We have now come to understand by the sloka that 650 years had elapsed from the time of Yudhishtira to the beginning of Sakyakala or the era of Gautama's Nirvana. It may here be stated that though Max Muller offers very fair reasons for fixing the date of Nirvana in 477* B. C., yet "there is perhaps no single point in the whole early history of India on which the chronicles of Ceylon and Further India are so distinct and unanimous than that Buddha died,—or as they express it, attained Nirvana—at the age of eighty years in the year 543 B. C."† The Dipawanso, the Pali chronicle of the fourth century A. D., computes by the era of Nirvana beginning in 544-3 B.C. But we are not concerned here with the question whether this date or Max Muller's date, 477 B.C., be the true date for the Pari-Nirvana of Buddha. It is enough to note that Burma, Siam and Ceylon are all unanimous in giving the former date and that such widespread unanimity of opinion cannot be expected unless the era of 544-3 B. C. had existed from a very long time. In my opinion, the date given by the

* Ancient Sanskrit Literature, p. 299.

† Bigandet's Life of Gautama, p. 323.

Buddhists of these three countries was the one current at the time of Garga. If the year 544-3 B. C. be incorrect, and the year 477 B. C. be the true date, we can only say that the error must have arisen long before the time of Garga who lived shortly after the lapse of three centuries from the Nirvana of Gautama Buddha. We are now in a position to understand the full force of Garga's statements that the Saptarshis moved by one Nakshatra in every hundred years, that they were in Magha when Yudhishtira reigned, and that 650 years had elapsed from that time to that of Buddha's Nirvana. These statements indicate to us that the coronation of Yudhishtira, and therefore the Mahabharata war, took place in the year (544 or 543 + 650, or) 1194-3 B.C.

There prevails in almost all parts of India what is generally known as the Brihaspati sixty-year cycle. The utility of such a small cycle lasting for about the lifetime of man, each year of which is designated by a special name, is patent to every one who has lived in India. To a European, its efficacy would best be demonstrated if he be asked how his countrymen would feel in case the twelve months of the year had no names given them, but had to be denoted by numerical figures. This cycle seems to have been in use in India from a very long time*. In commenting on Taittiriya Brahmana, I. 4. 10, Sayana says that this cycle comprised twelve of the ancient five-year cycles, which are so often referred to in the Vedic works† and in the Vedanga Jyotisha. Colebrooke thinks that the period of Jupiter (Brihaspati) was introduced by the ancient Hindus in conjunction with those of the sun and the moon in 'the regulation of the calendar, sacred and civil, in the form of the celebrated cycle of sixty years.'‡ As the sun and the moon take about five years to return both to the same position at the beginning of a year, a fact which gave rise to the cycle of the five years, known as *Samvatsara*, *Parivatsara*, *Idavatsara*, *Anuvatsara* and *Idvatsara* respectively, and as Jupiter makes a complete circuit of the heavens in about twelve years, it is evident that all the three heavenly bodies were expected to return to the same celestial region on the expiry of every sixty years. But in consequence of a correcter knowledge of Jupiter's motions, Northern India has been, for some-

* Warren's Kala Sankalita, p. 212.

† Taittiriya Samhita, V. 5. 7.; Taittiriya Brahmana, III. 4. 11; I. 4. 10; III. 10. 4. Taittiriya Aranyaka, IV. 19; Vajasaneya Samhita, XXVII. 45.

‡ Dutt's Ancient India, Vol. II, 242.

time past, expunging one year of the cycle in every $85\frac{65}{211}$ years, so that, after one such period, the name of the next year is left out and the name of the one following the next year taken to be the next year's name. As no such, evidently a comparatively recent, practice prevails in Southern India, the current year (April 1901 to April 1902), which is the year 'Pramadicha' in the North, is the year 'Plava' in the South.

At whatever time the cycle might have first originated, it appears to me that, when the names therefor were invented, the year of the Mahabharata War, the only famous epoch in the history of Ancient India, was named 'Prabhava,' the name of the first year of the cycle. But the date usually given by the orthodox for the war or for the beginning of the Kaliyuga does not correspond to the first year of the cycle. On the other hand, if we adopt the date given by Garga for the epoch of Yudhishtira, *i.e.* 1194-3 B. C., we find that the corresponding year of the Jupiter cycle for that date is 'Prabhava,' the name of its very first year.

We have already suggested that the Kaliyuga began at the winter solstice of the year 1177 B. C. We have also seen that, barring the argument based on Rajatarangini which gives us about

1190 B. C. for the war, our other lines of discussion point to 1194-3 B. C. as the probable date of the war. We shall now find that this date is further confirmed by the application of the principles of the Vedanga Jyotisha to certain statements contained in the Mahabbharata itself. We may here observe that these statements are not to be explained by the astronomical calculations of modern times, for these were unknown in the days of the war, but rather by the calculations of the Vedanga Jyotisha, which, though cruder, are better applicable to them, inasmuch as the Vedanga is the oldest Hindu astronomical treatise known to us and its astronomical details, as we have seen, relate to the beginning of the Kaliyuga.

In the Swargarohanika Parva of the Mahabharata, we are told that Yudhishtira having observed 'that the sun ceasing to go southwards had begun to proceed in his northward course' * set out to where Bhishma lay on his bed of arrows. After telling Yudhishtira, who had in the meantime arrived, that the winter solstice† had set in, Bhishma said ‡ :—

* Anusasanika Parva, CLXVII. 6.

† *Ibid.* v. 26.

‡ *Ibid.* v. 28.

माघोयं समनुप्राप्तः मासस्सौम्यो युधिष्ठिर ।
त्रिभागशेषः पक्षोयं शुक्लोभवितुमर्हति ॥

Babu Pratap Chunder Roy translated it thus:— "O Yudhishtira, the lunar month of Magha has come. This is again the lighted fortnight and a fourth part of it ought by this be over." Whatever historical weight may be attached to these statements, they may be at least taken to mean that the winter solstice then occurred on the expiry of the fourth part of the bright fortnight in the month of Magha, that is, on the fourth or the fifth day after new-moon. Nilakantha, the commentator of the Mahabharata, thinks that the expression त्रिभाग शेषः पक्षः denotes 'Magha Sukla Panchami'*, or the fifth lunar day in the month of Magha after new-moon. But Mr. Rangacharya† interprets the sloka to mean that the winter solstice occurred after the expiry of one-fourth part, not of the bright fortnight, but of the month of Magha, and thus he seems to think that the winter solstice took place on the eighth day after new-moon. He makes त्रिभागशेषः qualify मासः, the fourth word in the first line, instead of पक्षः, the next

* Com. on Bhishma Parva, XVII. 2.

† See his article in the *Indian Review* for October 1900.

following word. In the first place, the Anushtup verse, in which metre this and the adjoining slokas are written, generally consists of four quarters consisting of eight syllables each. "The fifth syllable of each quarter should be short, the sixth long, and the seventh alternately long and short." But though the fifth syllable in every other quarter in this verse and in all the quarters of the other verses is short, the fifth syllable of त्रिभागशेष:पक्षोयं alone is long owing to the addition of the 'visarga.' If the 'visarga' be left out, the rythm of the sloka becomes good enough. In that case, त्रिभागशेषपक्षः becomes one word and त्रिभागशेषे cannot but apply to पक्ष. But even without our resorting to this examination of the rythm of the verse, it strikes me that the novel interpretation of Mr. Rangacharya seems to be a forced one. The first line of the verse is complete by itself, as also the second line. Why should a word in the second line be taken to qualify a distant word in the first line instead of the next following word? The more natural interpretation appears to me therefore to be that given by the learned commentator of the epic and adopted by the translator thereof, namely, that the winter solstice happened on the fifth lunar day after Amavasya in the month of Magha

It may be observed that the Vedanga states * that at the beginning of every five-year cycle the winter solstice took place on a new-moon day with the sun and the moon together in Dhanishta Nakshatra. In verse 10, "we find an enumeration of the Nakshatras, or rather of the divinities presiding over the Nakshatras, in which the moon stands at the beginning of the ten Ayanas of the Yuga,"† that is, at the ten solstices of a five-year cycle. The ten Nakshatras are Sravishta, Chitra, Ardra, Purvaproshtapada, Anuradha, Aslesha, Aswayuj, Purvashada, Uttaraphalguni, and Rohini. ‡ But the Mahabharata states that the winter solstice occurred on the fifth lunar day after Amavasya. As according to the Vedanga§ the winter solstice always occurred with the sun in Dhanishta, the Amavasya referred to by the Mahabharata must have occurred with the sun and the moon in Sravana Nakshatra; and as the winter solstice occurred on the fifth day after this, the moon must have been, on the solstitial day, in or near Revati Nakshatra. According to the Jyotisha,|| this position could have occurred only at the

* Yajur recension of Vedanga Jyotisha, v. 5 and 8.
†Dr. G. Thibaut's Vedanga Jyotisha, p. 22.
‡ Verses 10, 32, 33 and 34.
§ Verses 5, 6 and 7.
|| Verses 10 & 32-34.

beginning of the fourth year of a five-year cycle, for it was then that the moon was in Aswayuja, next to Revati Nakshatra. The difference of this one Nakshatra is due to "the imperfections of the elements of the Jyotisha."* Thus we may infer that the winter solstice following the Mahabharata war, and just preceding† Bhishma's death, was the fourth of the five winter solstices of a five-year cycle. The particular five-year cycle in which the Mahabharata war took place appears to have been the fourth cycle previous to the beginning of the Kaliyuga in 1177 B.C., inasmuch as we have found that the Rajatarangini points to 1190 B. C., and that all other lines of discussion lead to 1194-3 B. C., as the probable date of the war. Consequently, the winter solstice shortly following the war was the fourth of the fourth five-year cycle preceding the commencement of the Kaliyuga, which began, like the five-year cycle, with a winter solstice and with the sun and the moon in Dhanishta Nakshatra. In other words, the Mahabharata war took place a little before the seventeenth winter solstice preceding the commencement of the Kaliyuga, or towards the end of the year 1194 B. C.

* Dr. G. Thibaut's Vedanga Jyotisha, p. 22.

† Anusasanika Parva, CLXVII, 26-28.

To summarize the arguments above set forth :— We were first enabled by the Vedanga Jyotisha to place the beginning of the Kali era approximately at about 1173 B. C.

Secondly; After enquiring into the date of Garga and of the Yavana invasion he spoke of, we noted that he fixed 'the end of the Yuga' for the retirement of the Greeks from Hindustan. From this statement we inferred that the Yuga, which ended sometime before 165 B. C., must have begun a few years before 1165 B. C.

Thirdly ; In explaining the figures given by the classical historians, we came to the conclusion that the Kaliyuga must have begun in 1177-6 B. C.

Fourthly ; The Malabar era furnished us with another authority for fixing the commencement of the Kali era in 1176 B. C.

Fifthly ; We found that if the Kali commenced at the winter solstice immediately preceding the year 1176 B. C., the details of the Mahabharata would lead us to place the war at the end of the year 1194 B.C.

Sixthly ; The tradition recorded in the Rajatarangini enabled us to fix the date of the war at about 1190 B. C.

Seventhly ; From a statement made by Aryabhata that the Rishis were in Magha in the year

1192 B. C., we inferred that the war might have taken place at about 1193 B. C.

Eighthly; The average duration of the reigns of the monarchs of the five foremost Powers of our hemisphere served to assist us in fixing the date of the war at about the year 1193 B. C.

Ninthly; From a sloka of Garga quoted in the Brihat Samhita, we inferred that the war occurred in the year 1194-3 B.C.

Tenthly; We also found that the first year of the Brihaspati cycle of sixty years actually corresponds, as may naturally be expected, to the date of the war as given by Garga, *i.e.*, 1194-3 B.C.

Eleventhly and lastly; We applied the elements of the Vedanga Jyotisha to a sloka contained in the Mahabharata, which fixes the day of the winter solstice occurring soon after the war, and concluded that the war should have taken place in the latter part of the year 1194 B. C.

Thus we find all this cumulative evidence derived from different sources converging to the result that the Kali era began at the winter solstice occurring at the end of 1177 B.C., and that the Mahabharata war took place at about the end of 1194 B.C. In arriving at these conclusions, we had the testimony of the only historian that India can boast of who lived in the twelfth century

A. D., of the greatest of the astronomers of India who flourished at the end of the fifth century A. D., of another brilliant astronomer who shone in the second century B. C., and of a versatile Greek historian who was also an ambassador at the court of the first great historic Emperor of India who reigned in the fourth century B. C. We had also the authority of the oldest astronomical work of India which claims to be a supplement to the Vedas, of the Kollam era which forms such a "splendid bridge from the old world to the new," and of the famous sixty-year cycle. We tested these conclusions by what we may call the common-sense process based on the lists of kings contained in the Puranas. During this long and tedious discussion we have also met and disposed of the arguments of those that give an earlier date.

We are particularly fortunate in having been able to find out so many reasons, for in the province of ancient Hindu chronology one is not often able to support one's opinions by more than a few authorities. As we proceed to discuss the significance and the origin of the system of the Chaturyugas, we shall also find further corroborative testimony to the correctness of the views I have herein ventured to put forth.

So far we have been treading on more or less firm ground. But if we attempt to fix the actual days of the year 1194 B.C. when the war may be supposed to have been fought, our authority will have to be the epic alone, by itself an unsafe guide. As has already been remarked, the Mahabharata is unfortunately neither the work of one author, nor of one age. Sir Monier Williams* thought that the compilation must have proceeded for centuries; and Weber says:—"Of the Mahabharata in its extant form, only about one fourth (some 20,000 slokas or so) relates to this conflict and the myths that have been associated with it; and even of this, two-thirds will have to be sifted out as not original, since in the introduction to the work (I. 81.) the express intimation is still preserved that it previously consisted of 8800 slokas only."† "But as to the period," says Weber, "when the final redaction of the entire work in its present shape took place, no approach even to direct conjecture is in the meantime possible; but, at any rate, it must have been some centuries after the commencement of our era".‡ Professor Macdonell, the author of the latest work on Sans-

* Indian Wisdom, Lect. XIII. 371.

† Indian Literature, p. 187.

‡ *Ibid.* p. 188.

krit Literature, assumes "that the original form of epic came into being about the fifth century B.C." * The late Professor Wilson † considered the probable date of the epic poem to be about the third century B. C.

It has been recently proposed to start an Indian Epic Society mainly for the purpose of sifting out the older portions of our incomparable epic. But the labours of such a Society, when brought to a successful termination, will not, in my opinion, militate against the authenticity of the texts we are presently to discuss. Most of these belong to the war portion of the Mahabharata, which, according to Weber, is recognisable as the original basis ‡ of the epic.

We have already referred to a sloka § of the epic which states that the winter solstice, which took place soon after the war, happened on the fifth day after new-moon in the month of Magha. In the very next preceding sloka, Bhishma tells Yudhishtira that he has been lying on his 'spiky bed' for the previous fifty-eight nights. It may be

* Sanskrit Literature, p. 285.

† Wilson's Introduction to Translation of Rig Veda, Vol. I., p. XLVII.

‡ Indian Literature, p. 187.

§ Anusasanika Parva, CLXVII, 28

observed that the bed referred to here consisted of the countless arrows that, shot from Arjuna's Gandiva, stuck into Bhishma's body. As soon as Bhishma fell down mortally wounded, the roar of the tenth day battle ceased; and on the warriors of both the sides assembling to have a look at the wounded soldier, he asked for a pillow to match his heroic 'bed.' "The kings standing there then fetched many excellent pillows that were very soft and made of delicate fabrics," seeing which Bhishma "said with a laugh, 'These, ye kings, do not become a hero's bed.' "* Arjuna alone understood the intentions of his grandsire and immediately provided a pillow made of three well-placed arrows to the immense satisfaction of the veteran warrior. Among Hindus it has for long been considered good for one's future state, for death to occur in the period between the winter and summer solstices. The grand old Bhishma did not allow the arrows sticking into his body to be removed lest he might die before the commencement of the auspicious period, but rather preferred to suffer the excruciating pain, to which one with a less magnificent *physique* would have speedily succumbed. So firm was the indomitable will of this stern warrior, this noblest

* Bhishma Parva, CXXI.

flower of ancient chivalry, that he cared little for the terrible agony of these fifty-eight nights and more. How remarkable was the power of religious conviction in those early heroic times !

The war is expressly stated in the epic* to have lasted for eighteen consecutive days. Moreover, in the Dronabhisheka† Parva, Karna is said to have refrained 'from taking part in the war for the ten days' during which Bhishma was the generalissimo of the Kaurava army. In the last chapter of Drona Parva it is stated that 'Drona,' who was the next commander-in-chief, 'was slain after having fought dreadfully for five days.' Karna led the army ‡ for the succeeding two days, and on the night of the next§ day after Karna's death, the war was brought to an end. When Yudhishtira was lamenting the death of Ghatotkacha on the fourteenth night of the war, Vyasa is said to have told Yudhishtira that 'in five days the earth would fall under his sway.'‖ From these references also it is clear that the war continued for eighteen consecutive days.

* Asramavasika Parva, X. 30.

† Sections II and V.

‡ Karna Parva, I. 15.

§ Salya Parva, I. 10—13.

‖ Drona Parva, CLXXXIV, 65.

As Bhishma was mortally wounded on the tenth day of the war, as the war lasted for eight days more, and as Bhishma is reported* to have stated on the day of the winter solstice that he remained on his bed of arrows for fully fifty-eight nights, the interval between the end of the war and the solstitial day was fifty days. As a matter of fact, this very † number of days is stated as the period of the stay of the Pandavas in the city of Hastinapura, which they entered on the next‡ day after the war, until they set out on their last visit to Bhishma on the day of the winter solstice. The epic says: "The blessed monarch (Yudhishtira) having passed fifty nights in Hastinapura recollected the time indicated by his grandsire (Bhishma) as the hour of his departure from this world. Accompanied by a number of priests, he then set out of the city, having seen that the sun ceasing to go southwards had begun to proceed in his northward course."§ After Yudhishtira reached Bhishma,

* Anusasana Parva, CLXVII. 26 and 27.

† *Ibid.* 5 and 6.

‡ Stri Parva, XXVII. Santi Parva, XLI and XLV. The Pandavas desired to pass the period of mourning which extended for a month outside Hastinapura (Santi Parva, I. 2); but their intention seems not to have been carried out.

§ Pratap Chunder Roy's Translation: Anusasanika Parva, CLXVII. 5 and 6.

the latter addressed him in these words: "The thousand-rayed maker of the day has begun his northward course. I have been lying on my bed here for eight and fifty nights."* We may therefore conclude that the winter solstice took place on the fifty-first day from the close of the war.

On the next† day after the close of war, Sri Krishna and the Pandavas paid a visit to the dying Bhishma, whom Sri Krishna addressed in the following words:—"Fifty-six days more, O Kuru Warrior, art thou going to live."‡ One need not be misled by the prophetic nature of this expression and declare it to be of no historic value. It might well have been a fact and put in the form of a prophecy by the compiler of the epic. But it may be asked how Bhishma could have lived fifty-six days after the close of the war, if only fifty days had elapsed from that time to the winter solstice when Bhishma hoped to give up his life-breath. But the explanation appears to me to be simple enough: though the winter solstice occurred fifty days after the close of the war, Bhishma does not seem to have

* *Ibid.* 26 and 27.

† Stri Parva, XXVII. Santi Parva, XLI. XLV. and LII.

‡ Rajadharmanusasana Parva, VI. 10.

died on the solstitial day, when the arrows were extracted from his body, but appears rather to have lingered on till the sixth day after the winter solstice. We have seen that the solstice took place then on the fifth lunar day after new-moon in the month of Magha. It was on the sixth day from this, that is, on Magha Sukla Ekadasi, that Bhishma, "that pillar of Bharata's race," seems to have "united himself with eternity." Tradition asserts that Bhishma died on this very day, and our almanacs even now make note of the fact and call the day by the name of "Bhishma Ekadasi." To this day, death on the eleventh lunar day of the bright fortnight of the month of Magha is held in great esteem, and next to that, death on such a day of any other month. Possibly the supposed religious efficacy rests on the memory of the day of the royal sage's death.

As the fifty-ninth day after Bhishma's fall corresponded to Magha Sukla Panchami, Revati or Aswini Nakshatra,* the day of Bhishma's overthrow, which took place on the tenth day of the war, happened, in accordance with the principles of the Vedanga,† on Margasirsha Sukla Panchami, in Dhanishta Nakshatra; and the Amavasya preceding it happened on the fifth day of the war in Jyeshta

---

* *Ante*, pp. 83-4.

† Vedanga Jyotisha, Yajur Recension, V. 31.

Nakshatra. As a matter of fact, Dr. G. Thibaut * gives this very Nakshatra for the last Amavasya but two of the third year of a five-year cycle, which particular new-moon our Amavasya actually is. We may therefore conclude that the war began on the fourth Nakshatra preceding Jyeshta or in Chitra of the month of Karthica and ended in Rohini Nakshatra in Margasira month.

The Pandavas tried many milder means before they at last resorted to the arbitrament of war; they even proposed to sacrifice their interests to some extent, if war could thereby be averted. Sri Krishna was the last to be sent on a mission of mediation and he started for Hastinapura "in the month of Kaumuda, under the constellation Revati, at the end of the Sarad (autumn) season and at the approach of the Hemanta (dewy season)."† According to the commentator and also to the translator, Kaumuda is the Kartica month. As the latter half of autumn corresponds to the month of Kartica, we may be certain that the statement means that Sri Krishna left for Hastinapura in the Revati Nakshatra of the month of Kartica. His efforts at recon-

* Dr. G. Thibaut's booklet on Vedanga Jyotisha, p. 15—17, Amavasya No. 36.

† Udyoga Parva, LXXXIII, 7.

ciliation having been of no avail, he seems to have returned to the Pandava camp in Pushya Nakshatra, for, as soon as he left Hastinapura, Duryodhana asked his warriors immediately to march the army to Kurukshetra, "For to-day the moon is in the constellation of Pushya". A little before Sri Krishna's departure from Hastinapura, he proposed * to Karna:

सप्तमाच्चापि दिवसात् अमावास्या भविष्यति ।
संग्रामो युज्यतां तस्यां तामाहुश्शक्रदेवतां ॥

"In seven days will there be new-moon; let the war be begun on that day which, they say, is presided over by Indra." As the commentator says, "Sakradevatam" denotes the Jyeshta Nakshatra, which is presided† over by Indra. The verse therefore indicates that the approaching Amavasya was to happen in Jyeshta Nakshatra. This serves to confirm our inference drawn from other texts, that the Amavasya, which occurred on the fifth day of the war, took place in Jyeshta Nakshatra. But, to say that the new-moon would occur on the seventh day seems to be certainly wrong, for Krishna was speaking to Karna in Pushya Nakshatra and the Amavasya was said to occur in Jyeshta, the

* Udyoga Parva, CXLII. 18.

†Taittiriya Samhita, IV. 4. 10. Taittiriya Brahmana, I. 5. 2.

tenth Nakshatra from Pushya. Probably 'सप्तमात्' is an error for 'दशमात्.'

The war, however, did not begin in Amavasya as suggested by Sri Krishna, for, as we have seen, Duryodhana moved out his army to Kurukshetra on Pushya Nakshatra. The Pandavas * too seem to have marched out of Upaplavya on the very same Pushya. Both the contending parties were in such a hurry to march their armies to the battle-field, because Pushya Nakshatra was considered auspicious for such purposes. Yet, it was not possible to begin the actual fighting on the very same day. Much remained to be done before the armies could meet each other in battle array. If Sri Krishna returned from Hastinapura with the answer of Duryodhana on Pushya Nakshatra, it is reasonable to allow some time for the marching of troops, for the ground to be cleared, for the pitching of tents, for the divisions of the armies to be properly effected, and, most of all, for the allied princes to bring on their respective divisions to the field of battle. It appears to me that all these preliminary arrangements were gone through during the interval of the five days between Pushya and Chitra, in which Nakshatra the fighting actually began. But

* Salya Parva, XXXV. 10 and 15.

our epic says that both the parties were prepared for battle on the day when the moon had gone to the region of Magha. * The natural interpretation† of the expression is that on that day the moon was in Magha Nakshatra. In that case we have to suppose that though the armies were almost ready for war in Magha Nakshatra, the first shot, to use a modern expression, was not fired till after the lapse of three more days. The armies began their march to Kurukshetra in Pushya, were organized in effective divisions in Magha, and actually engaged in battle in Chitra. Or, it may be that 'Magha' is an error for 'Maghava.' The expression then would mean that the moon had entered the region of Indra, that is, the star Chitra presided over ‡ by Indra. If the emendation prove to be correct we have here another testimony to the correctness of our conclusion that the war began in Chitra Nakshatra.

It must be borne in mind that the epic was cast into its present form more than a thousand years after the date of the war. How many altera-

* Bhishma Parva, XVII.

† The commentator gives such a glaringly far-fetched interpretation, that we need not pause here to discuss it.

‡Taittiriya Samhita, IV. 4. 10. Taittiriya Brahmana, I.5. 2.

tions, additions, omissions and errors must there have been made during this vast period! There are many statements in the epic which conflict with one another, a circumstance which can be accounted for only on this historic basis.

One such conflicting statement occurs in the Gadayudha Parva. On the last day of the war Balarama returned to Kurukshetra from his pilgrimage to the banks of the Sarasvati, * whither he had gone on the eve of the war in utter disgust with this horrible fratricidal war. He said:—"Forty-two days have elapsed since I proceeded forth; I left on Pushya, I have returned in Sravana." † The epic states expressly that the Pushya Nakshatra on which Balarama went away on pilgrimage was the one ‡ on which the Pandavas set out of Upaplavya to the field of battle. It also certainly implies§ that the Sravana Nakshatra on which Balarama returned happened on the last day of the war. If these statements are to be taken as authentic, the obvious inference is that the war, which began with the marching of armies to

* The bed of this river is still visible near Kurukshetra and Thaneswar. Dutt's Ancient India, I. 62.

† Salya Parva, XXXIV. 6.

‡ Salya Parva, XXXV. 10—15. Udyoga Parva, CLVII. 16—35.

§ Salya Parva, LIV. 32.

Kurukshetra on Pushya, came to an end in Sravana forty-two days later. This conflicts directly with the natural inferences we have drawn from the other statements, namely, that the winter solstice occurred on Magha Sukla Panchami fifty days after the close of the war, that the war lasted for eighteen consecutive days, that the Amavasya which occurred on the fifth day of the war took place in Jyeshta Nakshatra, and that Sri Krishna left for Hastinapura on his errand of peace on Revati Nakshatra of Kartica month and returned to Upaplavya on the next following Pushya. To avoid such a contingency two explanations of this manifestly corrupt text are possible. We have either to suppose that the statements about Balarama's departure on the eve of the war and about his return on the last day thereof are spurious as being opposed to the united testimony of other texts, or that the verse under discussion requires a little emendation. In the former case the inference to be drawn from the sloka is that Balarama left for the Sarasvati in Pushya Nakshatra twenty-seven days before the march of troops on the next Pushya Nakshatra to the battle-field and that he returned to Kurukshetra in Sravana some days before the close of the war. If, however, the sloka is incorrect, we may best correct it by changing 'forty-two' into 'twenty-four'. If Balarama had left on pilgrimage in Pushya and returned on the last day of the war, that being the twenty-fourth from the day of his departure, the last day of the war would happen in Rohini, a result which is identical with the one we have already deduced from other texts. In that case the sloka, which now runs,

"चत्वारिंशदहान्यद्य द्वे च मे निःसृतस्य वै ।
पुष्येण संप्रयातोस्मि श्रवणे (श्रोणायां) पुनरागतः ॥,"

might then read :—

चतुर्विंशत्यहान्यद्य चासन्मे निःसृतस्य वै ।
पुष्येण संप्रयातोस्मि रोहिण्यां पुनरागतः ॥

There is one other conflicting verse which we shall briefly discuss. On the fourteenth night of the war there was a tremendous battle between the contending parties. It is hinted in the epic * that the moon rose up on that night after three-fourths part of it had expired. This is certainly a mistake; for the new-moon having taken place on the fifth day of the war, the moon should have disappeared below the western horizon about an hour and a half before three-fourths of the night were over. On the evening of the fourteenth day of the war, Arjuna's vow to kill

*Drona Parva, CLXXXV. 28 and 46—56; an CLXXXVII. 1.

Jayadratha having been fulfilled, the Kurus, burning with revengeful thoughts, continued the strife far into the night. The epic would have us believe that during the first half of the night a tremendous battle raged in total darkness resulting in the death of Ghatotkacha, that both the armies thereafter lay down to sleep for some time, and that on the rise of the moon at about three o'clock in the morning, both the sides recommenced their fighting. It is more probable that the war continued for as long as the moon was shining and that the armies rested when the moon had set. The poet was perhaps led to make this mistake by his anxiety to render the night sufficiently horrible for Rakshasa heroes to fight with their powers of illusion. For, it must be remembered that the Rakshasa Ghatotkacha on the side of the Pandavas and the Rakshasa Alayudha on the Kaurava side are represented as having made the night hideous by their powerful uncanny powers, which could be used effectively only in total darkness.

But, barring these two conflicting statements which too may be explained away, all other texts serve, as we have seen, to support our conclusion, We are told that the winter solstice happened on Magha Sukla Panchami, that the tenth day battle happened fifty-eight days before it, that Bhishma, who died on Magha Sukla Ekadasi, gave up the ghost fifty-six days after the close of the war, that a period of fifty days intervened between the end of the war and the winter solstice, that the war lasted for eighteen consecutive days, that the Amavasya, which occurred soon after the commencement of the war, happened in Jyeshta Nakshatra, that the armies began their departure to the field of battle in Pushya Nakshatra, and that Sri Krishna had proceeded to Hastinapura on his mission of mediation on the preceding Revati Nakshatra in the month of Kartica. All these point but to one conclusion, namely, that the war, which lasted for eighteen consecutive days, concluded on the fifty-first night before the winter solstice.

At present the winter solstice falls on the 21st of December. The Gregorian system, which is the basis of the calendars of all Europe, except Russia, Greece and Turkey, "involves an error of less than a day in 3524 years".* As the war took place in 1194 B.C., or 3094 years ago or 2776 years before the calendar was last corrected by Pope Gregory XIII, we may be

* B J. Hopkins's Astronomy, p. 68.

certain that the winter solstice which occurred on the fifty-first day after the close of the war, would have happened, as now, on the 21st of December (New Style). We may therefore conclude that the War commenced on the 14th of October, and was brought to a close on the night of the 31st of October, 1194 B.C. Whether or not this precise date, based as it is on data furnished by the Mahabharata alone, proves to be acceptable to the critical eye of a historian, we may at least be sure that the War took place in the latter part of the year 1194 B. C.

CHAPTER III.

THE FOUR YUGAS.

WE have stated in the preceding chapters that the Kaliyuga commenced at the winter solstice occurring in the latter part of the year 1177 B. C., and that it was originally a period of one thousand years. It is apparent that these propositions are at conflict with the orthodox opinion which makes the Yuga begin in 3102 B. C. and last for 432,000 years. How has this popular belief come about? Is it possible to find a rational explanation for this variance? We shall endeavour to discuss these questions in the course of this chapter and the next; and if we succeed in finding satisfactory solutions therefor, we may then be able to understand a little better the Chronology of Ancient India.

The Vishnu Purana (I. 3.) enumerates the following divisions of time:—" Thirty Muhurtas make a day-and-night of human beings and a like number of day-and-nights makes a month of two Pakshas (fortnights). Six months make an Ayana (the period between the solstices), and two Ayanas constitute the year. The southern Ayana (the period between the summer and winter solstices) is a night, and the northern Ayana (the period between the winter and summer solstices) is a day, of the Gods. Twelve thousand divine years, of 360 such day-and-nights each, constitute the four yugas, Krita, Treta and the like. Know the manner of their distribution : the Kritayuga comprises 4,000 years ; the Tretayuga, 3,000 years ; the Dwaparayuga, 2,000 years ; and the Kaliyuga, 1,000 years. Thus those that know the past have declared. The period that precedes a yuga is called 'Sandhya,' which comprises as many hundred years as there are thousands in the yuga ; and the period which comes after a yuga is called 'Sandhyamsa,' which lasts for a like period. The intervals between these Sandhyas and Sandhyamsas are known as the yugas called Krita, Treta, and the like. The Krita, Treta, Dwapara and Kali go to constitute the Chaturyuga, a thousand of which make a day of Brahma. There are fourteen Manus in a day of Brahma."

The Surya Siddhanta (ch. I) also speaks of the same divisions of time. According to it,

The Kaliyuga with its Sandhya and Sandhyamsa consists of	432,000 years;
The Dwaparayuga do. ...	864,000 ,,
The Tretayuga do. ...	1,296,000 ,,
The Kritayuga do. ...	1,728,000 ,,
Thus a Mahayuga consisting of these four yugas comprise...	4,320,000 ,,
71 such Mahayugas with an additional Sandhya, at the close, of 1,728,000 years make one Manwantara of	308,448,000 ,,
Fourteen such Manwantaras with another Sandhya, at the beginning, of 1,728,000 years constitute one Kalpa of ...	4,320,000,000 ,,
Two Kalpas make a day-and-night of Brahma of ...	8,640,000,000 ,,
360 such day-and-nights make one Brahma's year of ...	3,110,400,000,000 ,,
100 such years constitute his life-time of	311,040,000,000,000 ,, ;

and there have been and will be many such Brahmas in the eternity of time.

This gigantic attempt to scale the ladder of Time is made also in almost all the Puranas and the astronomical Siddhantas, none of which however, as they now exist, can safely be assigned, as will be seen later on, to a date earlier than the fifth century A. D. But the Manusmriti and the

Mahabharata, both of which give a different account of the Yugas, are decidedly of an earlier date. Sir William Jones placed Manu between 1250 and 500 B. C.; and Schlegel was content with 1,000 B. C. Professor Duncker gives 600 B. C., and Wilson and Monier Williams, 500 B. C. Johaentgen gave 500-350 B.C., and the late Justice Mr. Telang, about 200 B. C. Dr. Burnell fixes 500—200 B. C. for the older prose code, out of which, according to him, the present metrical redaction arose between 100 and 500 A.D. Dr. Buhler, the learned translator of Manu in the Sacred Books of the East Series, states that this "estimate of the age of the Bhrigu Samhita (our metrical code), according to which it certainly existed in the second century A.D., and seems to have been composed between that date and the second century B.C., agrees very closely with the views of Professor Cowell and Mr. Talboys Wheeler." * As regards the Mahabharata, we have already given the various dates assigned to it by different scholars, all more or less pointing to the beginning of the Christian era for the work in its present shape. The opinion of Professor Macdonell on this point seems to me

* Introduction, p. CXVII.

to be very fair. He observes that the epic itself relates (1. 81.) that originally it consisted of 8,800 slokas only and then increased to 20,000 and 100,000 verses successively. He believes that the epic existed in an earlier form consisting of about 8,800 verses as early as the fifth century B.C., and that there was an extension 'after 300 B.C. and by the beginning of our era,' when the Yavanas, Sakas and Pahlavas are mentioned in it for the first time. He continues :— * "There is an inscription in a land grant dating from 462 A.D. or at the latest 532 A.D., which proves incontrovertibly that the epic about 500 A.D. was practically of exactly the same length (100,000 slokas) as it is stated to have in the survey of contents given in Book I., and as it actually has now.* * It is only reasonable to suppose that it had acquired this character at least a century earlier, or by about 350 A.D.* * We are already justified in considering it likely that the great epic had become a didactic compendium before the beginning of our era."

In his monumental Lexicon, Roth states that "according to the earlier conception stated in Manu and Mahabharata, the four yugas, Krita, Treta, Dwapara and Kali, with their mornings and even-

* Sanskrit Literature, p. 287.

ings, consisted respectively of no more than 4,800 3,600, 2,400 and 1,200 ordinary years of mortals." We find it stated in the Mahabharata (Vana Parva, ch. 188) :—"Four thousand years have been said to constitute the Kritayuga. Its dawn also, as well as its eve, hath been said to comprise four hundred years. The Tretayuga is said to comprise three thousand years and its dawn, as well as its eve, is said to comprise three hundred years. The yuga that comes next is called Dwapara and it hath been computed to consist of two thousand years. Its dawn as well as its eve is said to comprise two hundred years. The next yuga called Kali is said to comprise one thousand years, and its dawn, as well as its eve, is said to comprise one hundred years. When the Kaliyuga is over, the Kritayuga begins. This period of 12,000 years is called by the name 'Yuga.' One full thousand of such Yugas would constitute a day of Brahma. * * In the Kaliyuga, the Brahmanas will abstain from sacrifices and the study of the Vedas. * * Then will rule over the earth many Mlechcha kings.** The Audhas, the Sakas, the Pulindas, the Yavana kings ** will then rule over the earth." In this quotation we find that the periods for the yugas are much less than those given by the later Puranas and Siddhantas. According to the epic, the

Krita and other yugas last for 4,800, 3,600, 2,400 and 1,200 years respectively.

The passage serves also to show to us that it belonged to what Professor Macdonell calls the 'the second stage' in the history of the composition of the epic. We have already seen that a few Yavana or Græco-Bactrian kings were ruling over the northern parts of India from about 326 B. C., the date of Alexander's conquest of India, to about 165 B. C., and that they again invaded India at the time of Menander (144 B.C.) The Sakas first came into prominence about the time of Garga (165 B. C.); and the Yuehti tribe overran Bactria in about 126 B. C. and very shortly after invaded Northern India.* History does not know of any Yavana or Saka king *ruling* over Hindustan anterior to the dates given above. It obviously follows that the passage in question dates from a time not earlier than the first century before Christ.

The Manusmriti, which offers many striking similarities† to the Mahabharata, states (I. 69-71.) that the Krita, Treta, Dwapara and Kali yugas with their respective twilight periods consist

* Duff's Chronology of India, pp. 15-19.

†Buhler's Manu, Introduction, pp. LXXXV and LXXXVI; Telang's Introduction to Bhagavat Gita, in Vol. VIII of Sacred Books of the East Series.

of 4,800, 3,600, 2,400 and 1,200 years and that "this period of 12,000 years is called the yuga of the Devas." The original passage runs thus:

एतत् द्वादशसाहस्रं देवानां युगमुच्यते ॥

Though it has been given a forced interpretation by later commentators, it is evident that the most natural meaning is the one given above. As our metrical Smriti was composed, according to Dr. Buhler, between the 2nd century B. C. and the 2nd century A. D., we may take it that this passage dates from about the first century B. C. Thus we find two passages, one in the Epic and the other in the Smriti, both dating back to the first century B. C., which assign only 12,000 years to the four yugas. As stated by Dr. Roth, neither of the passages, if interpreted naturally, leads us to suppose that the years for these yugas are other than ordinary human years. Says Mr. W. J. Wilkins* :—" It should be noticed that the immense duration of the ages, as quoted above from the Vishnu Purana, is peculiar to the Puranas. In the text of the Mahabharata, 'no mention is made of the years comprising the different yugas being *divine years*.'†"

The mention of 'divine years' leads us naturally to a consideration of their nature and duration.

* Hindu Mythology, p. 297.
† Muir, O. S. T., I. 48.

It is stated in the Taittiriya Brahmana (III. 9. 22. 1.) that "one day of the Devas is a Samvatsara (human year)." The Suryasiddhanta, the Vishnu Purana and a number of other works refer to the same idea. The Vishnu tells us that "the period between the summer and winter solstices is a night, and that between the winter and summer solstices, a day of the Gods." This idea seems to have been derived from the old geographical notions current in Ancient India and recorded in the Mahabharata *and the Puranas. According to them, the mountain Meru was located in the middle of the Universe, round which the sun, the moon, the planets and the stars were said to revolve. The Dhruva Nakshatra or the Pole Star was said to shine just above its summit. "The world is here represented as consisting of seven concentric islands separated by different oceans. The central island, with Mount Meru in the middle, is Jumbudwipa of which Bharatavarsha," † or India, is the main division. The Meru was so lofty that the Himalayas were said to bear no comparison to it. What then was this gigantic Meru? The description of it leads one to conclude that it was no other than the northern hemisphere of our

* Bhishma Parva, VI—IX.
† Macdonell's Sanskrit Literature, p. 300.

round World, which certainly resembles the form of a mountain pointing to the North Pole and round which the celestial bodies undoubtedly appear to move. Our astronomers have made the point clear by telling us that "the equatorial line Bhuchakra divides the earth into Sumeru and Kumeru, the northern, and the southern, hemisphere. The northern hemisphere ends at 'Uttara Dhruva' or the North Pole, and the southern at 'Dakshina Dhruva' or the South Pole." At the North Pole is the top of the Meru where the Devas are supposed to live, and at the South Pole are said to reside Asuras, Pitris, and the God of Death.

It is very possible that the idea that the golden summit of Meru is the residence of the Devas (Shining Ones) originated in a faint recollection of the earliest history of the Aryan races, who must have, long before their dispersal towards the South and the West, resided somewhere in the northern latitudes near the Arctic regions, where the *Aurora Borealis*, which stirred Dr. Nansen's imagination so deeply in his expedition to the 'Farthest North,' plays such fantastic tricks. This wonderful display of the Northern Lights, for a long time the theme of scientific discussion, seems to have been easily disposed of by the primitive Aryan patriarchs as the golden abode of the '*Devas*,' a word coming from the root '*div*,' to shine, and having its counterparts in the Latin '*Deus*,' and in the English 'Divinity.' Even now if an unsophisticated person, uninfluenced by the scientific scepticism of the age, were suddenly to be transported to those dismal regions, would not his heart throb at the magnificent sight of that wonderful phenomenon? Nay, more, he would attribute that every recurring, ever vanishing, spectacle to the finger of God, to some divine agency. How much more must the simple forefathers of the Vedic Bards, who delighted in personifying and worshipping every element or object in Nature, have felt the 'divinity' of that remarkable scene!

Those frigid regions have only one long day and one equally long night during the course of a year. * As long as the sun is above the Equator, the North Pole enjoys its day and the South Pole passes through its night. If the sun appears to go south of the Equator, the North Pole is dark and the South Pole is bright. For the hypothetical Devas inhabiting the summit of Meru, the day lasts for as long as the sun is in the north of the Equator, or for six months; and the night lasts for the other six months of a year. In other words, the period between the vernal and autumn-

* Ball's Elements of Astronomy, pp. 139-149.

al equinoxes represents the day, and that between the latter and the former, the night, of those who may be said to reside, like the Devas, near the North Pole.

But we are told by the Vishnu Purana and the Surya Siddhanta that the Uttarayana, or the period between the winter and summer solstices, is a day, and that the Dakshinayana, or the interval between the summer and winter solstices, a night of the Gods. As Mr. Tilak points out,* Uttarayana and Dakshinayana, or as they seem anciently to have been known, the Devayana and Pitriyana, originally denoted the periods between the equinoxes and not those between the solstices. As the year originally commenced with the Devayana which was its first half, it is clear that when the beginning of the year was changed, shortly before the Mahabharata War, from the time of the vernal equinox to that of the winter solstice, the Devayana or Uttarayana also commenced with the new beginning of the year at the winter solstice. Thus the Uttarayana, instead of denoting the period when the sun was *in* the north, came subsequently to signify the period when the sun was proceeding *to* the north.

We therefore find that the belief that one hu-

* Orion, pp. 23-27.

man year constitutes a day-and-night of the Devas can be traced to the old geographical notions prevalent in India. As, according to old Hindu ideas,* the year consisted of 360 days only, a Deva year would last for 360 of their day-and-nights, or 360 human years. While the Manusmriti and the Mahabharata give 1200 ordinary *human* years for the Kaliyuga, the later Puranas and Siddhantas assign to it 1200 *divine* years, or 432,000 ordinary human years.

But even this period of 1200 ordinary years which were allotted to the Kaliyuga at about the first century B. C. consisted of 1000 years for the yuga proper and 200 years for its Sandhya (twilight) periods. On its face it is apparent that the Sandhya period did not form part of the original duration of the yuga itself. The Mahabharata says, 'The next yuga, called Kali, is said to comprise one thousand years, and its dawn as well as its eve, is said to comprise one hundred years.' It may be properly asked why this distinction is made between the yuga and its Sandhyas, when practically there is none at all between them. It might as well have been stated all at once that the Kali lasted for 1200 years. The Vishnu Purana also is to the same effect.

* Rig Veda Samhita, I. 164. 11 and 48.

"The Kritayuga comprises 4,000 years; the Treta, 3,000; the Dwapara, 2,000; and the Kali, 1,000. *Thus those that know the past have declared.* The period that precedes a yuga is called Sandhya * * and the period which comes after a yuga is called Sandhyamsa, which lasts for a like period. *The intervals between these Sandhyas and Sandhyamsas are known as the yugas called Krita, Treta and the like.*" If then the intervals only between the Sandhyas were known as the 'Yugas,' it obviously follows that the Kali, Dwapara, Treta and Krita 'Yugas' were thought by those 'that knew the past' to have lasted for 1,000 2,000, 3,000 and 4,000 years respectively, and that the Sandhya periods did not form part of the duration of the 'Yugas.' If the Kaliyuga had indeed been from the very first considered to be a period of 1200 years, no such unnecessary distinction as that drawn between the Yugas and their Sandhyas would probably have been made. As therefore the Sandhya periods were later additions, it is also apparent that those who brought them first into existence would not all at once state, for instance, that the Kali would last for 1200 years, for that would imply a want of due respect for the old belief that the Kali was a period of 1000 years, but would rather suggest that the Kaliyuga lasted for 1000 years and its Sandhyas for another period of 200 years.

We have also a *vaidik* authority for the contention that the Sandhya periods were not originally in existence. It may be observed here that all genuine Vedic works are much earlier in date than either the Epic or the Dharmasastra. In the Atharva Veda Samhita (VIII. 2. 21.), it is stated: शतं तेऽयुतं हायनान्द्वे युगे त्रीणि चत्वारि कृण्मः ॥ *i. e.*, "We allot to thee a hundred, (nay) ten thousand years, two, three, (or even) four yugas." Muir thinks that "we may with probability assume that the periods here mentioned proceed in the ascending scale of duration," and that "two yugas, and perhaps even one yuga, must be supposed to exceed ten thousand years." * It is very true that we have here an ascending scale of duration and that two yugas are decidedly meant to exceed 10,000 years. But with the greatest respect for so high and learned an authority, I venture to submit that *one* yuga is not intended here to exceed 10,000 years; for in that case the passage would run thus: "We allot to thee a hundred, (nay) ten thousand years, *one*, two,

* Original Sanskrit Texts, I. 46.

three, (or even) four Yugas." But as it is, the word 'one' is left out, purposely, as I venture to believe. In my opinion, one yuga was meant to equal 10,000 years, neither less nor more, for the following reason. The yugas are called distinctly by their names, Krita, Treta, Dwapara and Kali, in the Aitareya Brahmana (VII. 15.), a work of nearly the same date as that of the Atharva Samhita; and whereas the Gopatha Brahmana (I. 28) refers to the Dwapara age, the Mundaka Upanishad (I. 2. 1) mentions the Treta yuga in a distinct manner. The word 'yuga' in the passage quoted above from the Atharva Veda must therefore denote one of these four yugas, or a Chaturyuga comprising all of them. But it cannot signify the Kaliyuga, because the scale being in an ascending order of duration, 'two yugas' must exceed ten thousand years, whereas two Kaliyugas last, according to the evidence of the Smriti and the Epic, only for 2,400 years at the utmost. Neither does the word 'Yuga' refer to the Dwapara, Treta or Krita yugas, for two such yugas cannot exceed 4,800, 7,200, or 9,600 years respectively at the utmost. Therefore the word 'Yuga' should denote the duration of a Chaturyuga, which is a period of 10,000 or 12,000 years according as we exclude or include the Sandhya periods. But the 'Yuga' does not constitute the larger period, for, as we have already seen, in that case the word 'one' would have been inserted before 'two.' Thus, if we grant, as we must, that the scale is in an ascending order of duration, we arrive at the probable result that the 'Yuga' means a Chaturyuga lasting for 10,000 years. As a matter of fact, we have already quoted a passage from the Manusmriti wherein a Chaturyuga is called 'a yuga of the Devas,' and another from the Mahabharata in which it is called by the simple name of 'yuga.' It is therefore extremely probable that the word 'Yuga' in the passage quoted above from the Atharva Samhita expresses the same idea as the very same word does in the passages extracted above from the Dharma Sastra and the Epic, *i.e.*, a Chaturyuga. As the passage in the Atharva Veda is addressed to a deity, His 'Yuga' would be a 'Yuga of the Devas' consisting of 10,000 years. Just as among mortals, there are four yugas, the first or Kali lasting for 1000 years, the next previous or Dwapara for twice that period, the Treta and Krita for thrice, and four times that duration respectively, so also, as being a Deva, he was allotted first a yuga of 10,000 years, then successively, two, three and four such yugas. This appears to me to be the meaning intended. If therefore a Chaturyuga lasted for 10,000 years, the Kali, Dwapara, Treta and Krita should have lasted only for 1,000, 2,000, 3,000 and 4,000 years respectively.

We find therefore that at the time of the compilation of the Atharva Veda Samhita, the Kaliyuga was supposed to last for 1000 years, that at the time of the composition of our Metrical Manusmriti and of the second redaction of the Mahabharata in 20,000 slokas, the Kaliyuga with its Sandhya and Sandhyamsa was thought to be a period of 1200 years, and that since the date of the Vishnu Purana and Surya Siddhanta, as we now find them, the Kali has been considered to last for 1200 × 360, or 432,000 years. What then led to the changes successively made in the durations of the yugas?

We have already proved that the Kaliyuga and the Kollam Andu commenced in 1177—76 B. C. If the Kali was originally a period of 1000 years, we find that the Kali corresponded exactly to the first Kollam cycle. Both came to an end in 177—76 B. C. It has been seen that Gargacharya, who was then living, said with reference to the Bactrian invaders who left India in about 165 B. C., that they retired 'at the end of the yuga'.

Consequently the yuga which came to an end at about 165 B. C., was certainly the Kali of one thousand years, or the first cycle of what has since come to be known as the Kollam Andu.

From this time forward the Kollam Andu has a history of its own. The forefathers of some at least of the modern Namburis seem to have separated from the main body of the Aryan people not long after this time. They seem to have settled first in the Andhra country and, after the lapse of a few more centuries, to have permanently fixed their residence in the fertile tracts of rainy Malabar. Says Mr. V. Nagam Aiya in his report on the Census of Travancore (I. p. 654):—"The bulk of them (the Brahman colonists of Malabar) came of course from the region between the Krishna and the Godavari rivers," which, having no natural advantages, has "a poor soil, inhospitable climate, and a poverty-stricken population, constantly devastated by long droughts and severe famines. This land naturally, therefore, supplied Parasurama with the largest number of his colonists. The Namburis themselves believe that most of them came from the land lying between the two great rivers, the Krishna and the Godavari. Tradition points to the same theory, and the ancient books on Kerala confirm the popular belief, the accuracy of which may be verified by a careful observer. There are so many points of similarity, large and small, between the Namburis and their prototype residents of the Telugu country from which they are said to have come." Mr. Nagam Aiya then proceeds to enumerate fourteen such 'points of similarity,' the cumulative effect of which is certainly favourable to his conclusion.

It need not be supposed that the Aryans had no knowledge of India south of the Narmada in the second century B. C., for we find that even such an early work as the Aitareya Brahmana (VII-18) speaks of "certain degraded barbarous tribes, among them the Andhras." Baudhayana (6th century B. C.) mentions Kalinga, and Katyayana (4th century B. C.) speaks of Chola and Pandya. Asoka (3rd century B. C.) mentions the Cholas, Pandyas, Kalingas, and 'Keralaputra' in his inscriptions; and Apastamba himself (between the fifth and the third century B. C.) is said by Dr. Buhler to have belonged to the Andhra country. Megasthenes (300 B. C.) refers to the Kalingas, Andhras, and Pandae or Amazon country. Ptolemy (126—161 A.D.) makes one Chera King 'Kerebothros' rule over 'Karoura' (Karur). Dr. Buhler is therefore led to the conclusion that the Aryan conquest of South India took place 'long before the fourth century B.C.'*

It is thus apparent that when the little band of the forefathers of some at least of the modern Namburis saw the end of the yuga of 1000 years which commenced soon after the Mahabharata War, they followed it up by another cycle lasting for a like period, led no doubt thereto by the fact, which they seem to have faintly remembered, that two such yugas of one thousand years each had expired about the time of the Mahabharata War. By the time that this second cycle came to an end in 825 A. D., they had for some time been settled in Malabar. The third cycle, which began in 825 A. D., came therefore to be known as the Kollam Era, after the name of a famous town in Malabar.

The Kaliyuga had a quite different transformation among the main body of the Aryan people of India. It came to a close, as we have seen, in 177 B. C. But the old belief was that the Kritayuga of 4,000 years followed the Kaliyuga of 1,000 years. It must be remembered that the Krita has always been thought to be an age of transcendent purity, when, according to the Mahabharata (Vana Parva, CXLIX.), "Every

* Sacred Books of the East, Vol. II., Introduction.

one had religious perfection. ** There was then neither disease, nor the decay of the senses. There was no malice, no pride, no hypocrisy, no discord, no ill-will, no cunningness, no fear, no misery, no envy, no covetousness. ** All acts had reference *to the attainment of Brahma.*" The epic continues :—"In the Treta age, virtue decreased by a quarter and the God Narayana (who, in the Krita age, was white) assumed a red colour. Men practised truth and devoted themselves to religious rites. Sacrifices were introduced. * * Men then began to aim *at attaining objects*, which they obtained by performing religious acts and making gifts. ** In the Dwapara, virtue decreased by a half. Vishnu assumed a yellow colour and the Vedas became divided into four parts. * * Mostly *induced by passion*, men engaged in asceticism and gift. * * As the intellect deteriorated, few were devoted to truth. * * In the Kaliyuga, only one quarter of virtue remains. When this age appears, Kesava assumes a black colour. The Vedas, the Institutes, virtue, sacrifices and religious observances, *all fall into disuse.* Then excessive rainfall, draught, rats, locusts, * * diseases, lassitude, anger, deformities, natural calamities, anguish and fear of famine take possession of the world. * * The religious acts performed at the waning of this yuga produce contrary results."

As the Kali of 1000 years came to an end in 177 B. C., the golden age of Krita ought then to have come into existence. But the glorious state of things predicted for the Krita was so opposed to the state of morals and of society in 177 B. C., that learned divines in India must have keenly felt the difference between the sinful nature of their times and the ideal state of things which ought to prevail in the Krita age. Whereas according to the old beliefs recorded in the Mahabharata (Vana Parva, CXC.) the barbarian Mlechchas, the pest of India in the Kali age, must have ceased to exist in the Kritayuga, Buddhism, foreign invasions and barbarian influences were rampant in India during the second century B. C. So the questions to be solved at that time were whether the Krita really signified a golden age of religion and of virtue and whether the Kritayuga had actually set in. Orthodox India could never have brought itself to propose the first question as it would reveal a woeful lack of reverence for the scriptures of olden times. The second question, which also was not quite a safe one, was however not so dangerous. They therefore solved their difficulties in a manner characteristic of every conservative people who have to reconcile the dicta of the past with the actualities of the present. They supposed that the effects of the Kritayuga could not all at once change the influences of a thousand years of the Kali age. As in the physical world the darkness of the night is first removed by the mild influence of the dawn before the sun shows himself in all his glory, just as the morning twilight heralds the day and the evening twilight precedes the night, so in the moral world, there ought to be a transitional period when the effects of both the Kali and Krita yugas would merge into one another. This necessary interval of transition was called the Sandhya (junction) period and as the Kali lasted for 1000 years, the 'twilight' periods preceding and succeeding it were each made to extend for an additional tenth part of the yuga, a proportion which seems to have been borrowed from the daily phenomena of morning and evening twilights. Krishna Pandita, the author of a Bhashya on Sandhyavandana, quotes with approval the following two slokas from some unnamed Smriti :—

अहोरात्रस्य यस्संधिस्सूर्यनक्षत्रवर्जितः ।
तत्रसन्ध्यामुपासीत सायंप्रातस्समाहितः ॥
उदयात्प्राक्तनी संध्या घटिकात्रयमुच्यते ।
सायं संन्ध्या त्रिघटिका अस्तादुपरिभास्वतः ॥

So also in the Ahnika Kanda of Smritimuktaphala, Vaidyanatha Dikshita says:—

यत्तु प्रातस्सन्ध्या त्रिनाडीस्यात् साय सन्ध्या तथाविधेति स्मरणं ॥

These slokas tell us that the morning and evening Sandhya prayers are to be performed at the Sandhi (junction) of the day and night, when neither the sun nor the stars are visible, that the morning Sandhi extends to three Ghatikas (3 × 24 minutes) before sunrise and that the evening Sandhi lasts for a like period after sunset. As the period between sunrise and sunset in India is about 12 hours on an average, and as each of the two Sandhyakalas lasts for three ghatikas, or for 1 hour and 12 minutes, according to these recognised authorities, the Sandhyakala is exactly one-tenth of the duration of a day of 12 hours. These Sandhya prayers date from a time not later than that of the Taittiriya Aranyaka, in which they are elaborated. It is therefore probable that this determination of the time for their performance may have been made at a pretty early period.

It is interesting to note that exactly the same period is given by modern astronomers for the twilights. Says Sir Robert Ball in his Elements of Astronomy (pp. 154-5):— "The dusk is thus usually visible until the centre of the sun has been carried by the diurnal motion to a perpendicular distance of 18° below the horizon. Similarly the earliest glimpses of dawn may be caught when the sun, in his approach to the horizon, has attained a distance of only 18° therefrom." In places, like India, which are located near the equator, "before sunrise the sun will ascend perpendicularly to the horizon, and after sunset it will descend perpendicularly below it. The twilight will therefore continue in this special case during the time when the sun moves through an arc of 18° on the celestial sphere, in virtue of the apparent diurnal motion. As the diurnal motion completes its revolution in twenty-four hours, a point on the equator which moves through 360° in one revolution must move through 15° in one hour. To move through an arc of 18°, a time of 1 hour 12 m. will therefore be required. Hence it appears that under the circumstances we have described the twilight at dusk and at dawn will last for a period of 1 hour, 12m."

This determination of the duration of the twilights appears to have been made use of in the fixing of the periods for the Sandhyakalas of the Yugas. As a day of 12 hours has two twilight periods, each lasting for 1h. 12m., *i.e.*, for one-tenth of the duration of a day, similarly the Kaliyuga of 1000 years came to have two Sandhyas, each lasting for 100 years. So also the Krita, Treta and Dwapara yugas were allotted proportionate Sandhya periods, namely, 800, 600 and 400 years respectively. It is not to be inferred that these Sandhya periods were added to the yugas just at the close of the Kaliyuga in 177 B. C. It would be unphilosophical to suppose that this contrivance was sought for and discovered immediately after the completion of the Kali. It would have taken some time for people to be thoroughly satisfied that the Kritayuga had not actually set in. Until it became evident that the effects of the old Kaliyuga still lingered on, they would not have been so bold as to innovate on old ideas. Moreover, Garga speaks of certain kings as ruling in Oudh after the destruction of the Yavanas 'at the end of the yuga,' a statement which necessarily leads to the inferences that Garga wrote his historical portion of his Siddhanta sometime after 'the end of the yuga' and that he still believed that the yuga lasted only for 1000 years. It therefore stands to reason that these Sandhya additions were effected a few decades later, say, in the first century before Christ. This date perfectly accords with that we have already given for the Manusmriti and the Mahabharata, both of which, dating from the first century B. C., refer to the twilight periods for the first time.

The description of the effects of the Kaliyuga, as contained in the 188th and 190th chapters of the Vana Parva of the Mahabharata is very graphic and it would be needless to reproduce it here. These chapters proclaim many times over that religion and virtue will disappear and that the barbarian Sakas, Yavanas, Balhikas and many others will devastate Bharatavarsha '*at the end of the Kaliyuga.*' It may be remembered that the Sakas, Yavanas and a few others were actually disturbing the peace of India in the first and the second century B. C. We may shrewdly guess from such statements that the end of Kali was supposed not to be far off. The Epic also tells us that the Kaliyuga would end " when the sun, the moon and Jupiter enter the constellation of Pushya (the nebulous Praesepes), at which time the clouds would incessantly shower rains, and stars and planets would again be propitious.** Abundance, prosperity, wealth and peace would be everywhere. Impelled by Time, a Brahmana named Kalki Vishungasha would then be born. He would possess great energy, intelligence, and prowess. He would be born at a village called Sambhala, in a blessed Brahman family. * * * He would exterminate all the low and despicable Mlechchas wherever they might be found," and the Krita yuga would then commence. The conjunction of these three heavenly bodies in the same celestial region generally takes place, as we have seen in the last chapter, once in every 60 years. If the compiler of the Mahabharata had a long period in mind to elapse before the end of Kali, he would not have chosen to denote the end of it by a conjunction which generally takes place once in every 60 years. It is therefore probable that he fixed the end of the Kali yuga at about the time of the next such conjunction. Moreover the prophecy regarding the birth of Kalki Vishungasha at Sambhala village seems to refer to some local belief current at the time. If the end of the Kali were to take place after the lapse of a long period, the name of the village also in which the incarnation was to take place would not perhaps have been given. All these circumstances tend to show that the Kali yuga was to come to a close very shortly after the first century B. C., the date of this portion of the Mahabharata.

The Kali yuga of 1200 years actually came to an end in 24 A. D. It was eagerly hoped that better times would dawn in Bharata Varsha at least after that critical epoch. If we have to guage aright the intensity of anxiety felt at that time, we have only to call back the slighter experiences we ourselves underwent barely three years ago. The 'five-thousandth year Pralaya' was on the lip of every Hindu and a mysterious significance was attached to it. We were also amused to find the ill-concealed solicitude of our Government to understand our feelings and beliefs in that anxious period. So also the approach of the 'millennium' was regarded with awe and anxiety during the times of Otto the Great and his imperial successor, the noble-minded Otto III.

But a better age did not dawn in 24 A. D. and the eager hopes of the people were not destined to be fulfilled. Far from there having been any sign of the Krita age, Buddhism was at its height and Brahmanism at its lowest ebb in India. Scepticism had come to prevail over orthodoxy. The greatest king of the time was Kanishka, a barbarian professing an atheistic creed. The fourth great council of Buddhism was then formulating its dogmas in the land of Vedic ritualism. Many Mlechcha kings were despoiling the north and the west of India. Instead of the Vedic religion coming back in its pristine glory, it was losing its most influential adherents through the proseletizing zeal of Buddha's creed. Could such a time, the Hindus seem to have asked themselves, be the beginning of the golden age? Were then the prophecies of the ancient sages to be thus falsified? These considerations seem to have sorely perplexed the minds of the orthodox Hindus of the first one or two centuries of the Christian era.

Then arose what we may call the Renaissance period in the history of India, a period of great activity in many branches of literature, arts, sciences and religion. In a long note added to the first edition of '*India, What can it teach us*,' Max Muller "tried to show that that period began about 400 A.D., and that the great break between the ancient Vedic and Buddhistic literature and the artificial Kavya literature was due to the inroads of the Scythians. He had fixed that literary interregnum as between the first century B. C. to at least the third century A. D." Professor Buhler controverted this opinion and showed that there were clear traces of the Kavya style in the inscriptions of the second century A. D. Max Muller replied by stating that "amongst the *literary* works (of the Kavya style) which we actually possessed, none could be safely referred to a date before about 300 A.D." Though scholars may not yet agree with Max Muller to the full extent of his opinions, yet they will concede, I have no doubt, that such a great impetus was given at that time to the cause of learning and literature, that it might well have merited the name of the Renaissance period. Hinduism had just then begun to revive* and to don its modern garments. The force of Buddhistic, Jain and Atheistic systems having weakened the strongholds of orthodox beliefs, this reactionary age set about to place the old dogmas and observances on a rationalistic basis. The coat armour of ancient Hinduism, battered as it appeared to be by the repeated onslaughts of opposing creeds, was then slowly patched up and tried to be rendered nearly impervious to the darts of reason or sentiment. An age of construction, of readjustment and re-arrangement of ancient beliefs, had now succeeded a destructive age of scepticism and of barbarian invasions. The pity of it was that reaction was carried a little too far to the verge of superstition, and the Puranas began to show not only a sectarian tendency, but also a taste for the marvellous and the extraordinary.

At this remarkable period in Indian History, the glaring absurdity of supposing the Kali yuga to have already come to an end must have been keenly felt. If the Kali of 1200 years had ended in 24 A.D., the

* Dr. Bhandarkar's article on the Social History of India in Chintamani's *Indian Social Reform*, p. 2.

Krita must have set in, which was not the case. As necessity has generally been the mother of invention, there arose an explanation, as ingenious as it was plausible, that the 1200 years allotted for the Kali were so many *divine* years, or 432,000 ordinary human years. Such a subtle explanation obviated the danger of the Kaliyuga coming again to a speedy end and thereby giving rise to fresh difficulties. It agreed well with the state of society at that time, which showed no signs of reverting to, but was receding away from, the ancient orthodox ideal. It served to preserve the authority of the older writings like the Mahabharata and the Manusmriti, both of which assigned 1200 years to the Kali age, and applied very well to existing circumstances. Moreover, the age of exaggerations had already commenced and the Puranas were beginning to distort facts into fabulous legends. Under such circumstances the extraordinary duration of the yugas was quite in keeping with the times.

It remains now for us to discuss the significance and the origin of the names of these different yugas. The word *yuga* comes from the root *yuj*, to join, and possibly it originally meant 'a collection of years.' Mr. Rangacharya, however, states that it "is both in meaning and etymology allied to the astronomical term *conjunction*." It seems to me that originally the word *yuga* could have had nothing to do with the astronomical phenomenon of 'conjunction,' for the obvious reason that the word is used in some of the earlier hymns of the Rig Veda, to the time of whose composition it may perhaps be preposterous to attribute such knowledge. It is more consistent with what we know of the state of society in those ancient times, that a *yuga*, 'age,' was then only a large division of time without reference to the motions of the celestial bodies. According to Muir, it frequently occurs in the Rig Veda "in the sense of age, generation or tribe." This scholar collects in his profound *Original Sanskrit Texts* (I. 45.) almost all the passages of the Rig Veda, wherein the word occurs. This ancient work speaks of *Yuge Yuge* 'in every age', *Uttara Yugani* 'future ages,' *Uttare Yuge* 'in a later age,' *Purvani Yugani* 'former ages.' *Yuga Jurna* 'former age,' *Manushya Yuga*, *Manusha Yuga* and *Jananam Yuga* all meaning 'human yuga,' *Devanam purvye Yuge* 'in a former yuga of the Devas,' *Devanam Yuge prathame* 'in the first yuga of the Devas,' *Devebhyah thriyugam pura* 'before three yugas from (or of) the Devas,' *Nahusha Yuga* 'the age of Nahusha,' and *Dasame Yuge* 'in the tenth yuga.' We learn from these extracts that, in the days of the Rig Veda, the word *Yuga* denoted a period of time which seemed to vary according as it was used in connection with human beings or the Devas.

We have already seen that the Atharva Veda Samhita speaks of the yugas in such a manner as to lead us to infer therefrom that at the time of its compilation a *Yuga* (chaturyuga) comprised ten thousand years. But for the first time in the literature of India, the words Krita, Treta, Dwapara and Kali occur in three nearly contemporaneous Vedic works, the Aitareya and Taittiriya Brahmanas and the Vajasaneya Samhita, all of which were compiled, like the Atharva Samhita, within about a century after the Mahabharata War.

It may be generally stated that the Samhitas are older* than the Brahmanas which are chiefly commentaries on the ritualistic portions of the former. Tradition, which in this case there is no reason to doubt, ascribes the compilation of the '*Thraividya*,' the three Samhitas of the Rik, Saman, and Black Yajur Vedas, to the time of Krishna Dwaipayana, under whose superintendence it seems to have been effected. As he was a contemporary of the heroes of the Mahabharata War, we may be sure that they took their original shapes at that time. But the Atharva Samhita and the

*Max Muller's Rig Veda, Vol. IV, Preface, V—VII.

Vajasaneya Samhita of the White Yajus seem to have come into existence a little, but only a little, later. Though the 'Atharvanas' are mentioned in the 30th book of the Vajasaneya Samhita, in the 11th, 13th and 14th books of the Satapatha Brahmana, in the 7th book of the Chhandogya Upanishad and in the 2nd and 8th books of the Taittiriya Aranyaka, yet the fact that even comparatively so late a work as our Manusmriti speaks of only three Vedas and that the Taittiriya Aranyaka assigns the Atharva Veda only a secondary position by inserting '*adesa*,' *i.e.*, the Brahmanas, between the three other Vedas and the Atharvangirasas,* shows that it had not attained the rank of a Vedic Samhita till long after the compilation of the three other Vedas. Even now in Malabar the name of "the fourth veda" is popularly applied, ludicrously enough, to the Khoran of the Mussalmans and not, as in the rest of India, to the Atharva Veda, a circumstance from which we may perhaps infer that the Namburi Brahmans originally knew, like the Manusmriti, only of three Vedas and separated from the rest of the Aryan folk before the Atharva Veda had attained the dignity of a Vedic Samhita; but this is by the way. At whatever time it might have been recognised as a

* Weber's Indian Literature, p. 149.

Veda, it is enough for our purpose to bear in mind that it is more recent than the three older Samhitas and that it is probably contemporaneous with the Vajasaneya Samhita in which it is referred to.

The Vajasaneya Samhita must have been compiled not long after the Mahabbharata War, for its compiler Yagnavalkya, the reputed pupil's pupil of Krishna Dwaipayana, was a celebrated divine, who is referred to in the Satapatha Brahmana (XIII.14) in the following connection. Yagnavalkya is asked by a rival, 'Whither have the Parikshitas (the four sons of Parikshit, the grandson of one of the Pandavas) gone?' He answers 'Thither where (all) Asvamedha sacrificers go.' "Consequently," says Weber in his *Indian Literature* (p. 126), "the Parikshitas must at that time have been altogether extinct. Yet their life and end must have been still fresh in the memory of the people, and a subject of general curiosity." Weber also says (p. 125): "The time when these last four (Janamejaya Parikshita, Bhimasena, Ugrasena, and Srutasena) lived cannot be considered as very distant from that of the Kanda (13th of the Satapatha Brahmana) itself, since their sacrificial priest Indrota Daivapa Saunaka (whom the Mahabharata, xii. 5595, also specifies as such) is once mentioned in it apparently as coming forward in opposition to Bhallaveya; while his own opinion, differing from that of the latter, is in turn rejected by Yagnavalkya." It may also be remembered that Yagnavalkya is said to have compiled his redaction of the Yajur Veda in a systematic manner as a protest against the diffuse and unmethodical Samhita of the Black Yajur Veda, where both the Mantra and Brahmana portions are jumbled together. We are therefore justified in placing the Vajasaneya Samhita and the Atharva Veda Samhita shortly after the War, say, within a century of its occurrence.

The Aitareya Brahmana also refers to Janamejaya Parikshita and is, according to Professor Macdonell, earlier than the Satapatha Brahmana, which, as we have seen, was written shortly after Janamejaya's time. Dr. Haug seems to consider the Aitareya to be one of the earliest of the Brahmanas,* whereas Professor Macdonell thinks it to be later than the Taittiriya and Panchavimsa† Brahmanas. As the Taittiriya Samhita, at all events in its original form, dates from the time of the War, the Taittiriya Brahmana, which is partly a commentary on, and partly a continuation of, the Taittiriya Samhita which it resembles so closely, must have been compiled soon after the War. Consequently it

*Aitareya Brahmana, Vol. II. p. 464.

†Sanskrit Literature, p. 203.

may be concluded that the Taittiriya and Aitareya Brahmanas, like the Vajasaneya and Atharva Samhitas, date from the first century after the War, or from the eleventh century B.C.

I have dwelt at such length on the dates of these Vedic works because we are thereby enabled to ascertain the time when the four yugas are first referred to in Sanskrit literature. The names of these yugas occur for the first time in the Aitareya Brahmana (VII-15), where it is said :—"Kali is lying, Dwapara is slowly shaking up, Treta is standing, and Krita is in full motion, (hence) wander on, wander on." As Muir points out, the very same idea is expressed in the Manusmriti (IX. 301-2) : "The Krita, Treta, Dwapara and Kali yugas are all modes of a king's action; for a king is called a Yuga. While asleep, he is the Kali ; waking, he is the Dwapara age ; intent upon action, he is the Treta ; moving about, he is the Krita." A slightly different rendering of the same comparison is found in the Mahabharata (III. CXC.), where Markandeya tells Yudhishtira ; "In the Krita age, everything was free from deceit and guile, avarice and covetousness. Virtue like a bull was among men with four legs complete. In the Treta, sin took away one of its legs and virtue had then (only) three legs. In the Dwapara, sin and virtue are mixed half and half. In the dark (Kali) age, virtue, being mixed with three parts of sin, lives by the side of men. Accordingly virtue is said to wait upon men with only a fourth part remaining." Dr. Haug explains the foregoing quotation from the Aitareya Brahmana in the following manner: " Sayana does not give any explanation of this important passage where the names of the yugas are mentioned for the first time. The four names are, as is well-known from other sources, names of dice used at gambling. The meaning of this *gatha* is: There is every success to be hoped; for the unluckiest die, the Kali, is lying, two others are slowly moving and half fallen, but the luckiest, the Krita, is in full motion. The position of dice here given is indicative of a fair chance of winning the game." That Dr. Haug's interpretation is quite inapplicable is the opinion of Drs. Muir, Weber, Roth, Strater, Wilson and Max Muller.* Moreover it is not correct to say that the names Krita, Treta, Dwapara, and Kali, are used here 'for the first time,' because we shall presently find that these names are used, though not in the same sense, in the Taittiriya Brahmana and the Vajasaneya Sambita, both of

* Muir's O. S. T., I. 48.

which are of the same, if not of an earlier, date. Says Mr. Rangacharya in his '*Yugas*' (p. 25):— "This passage has been variously interpreted, and it appears to me that we have here the myth concerning the Bull of Dharma so frequently related in the Puranas and the Mahabharata (III. 190). According to the Amarakosa, it can be shown that the Sanskrit word *Vrisha* means both *bull* and *virtue* (Dharma). * * A bull, when lying down, appears to be using one of its feet so as to press against the earth; when it tries to get up, two of its feet are seen to be applied to the earth; sometimes, when standing without motion, the animal may be seen to rest on only three of its feet; and, when walking and moving from place to place, it of course uses all four feet." It will be seen that this explanation is not on all fours with the passages quoted above from Manu and the Mahabharata, according to the latter of which, the bull has only one leg in the Kali, two in the Dwapara, three in the Treta, and its full complement of legs only in the Krita age. But it is possible that the double signification of '*Vrisha*' may have given rise to the ideas contained in all these three works. As '*Vrisha*' is dormant in the Kali by reason of its possessing one leg only, but is in full motion in the Krita age when it has all its four legs, so also Rohita, to whom the passage of the Aitareya Brahmana is addressed, is advised to wander on like the '*Vrisha*' in the Kritayuga, and not to go back to his father Harischandra to be inactive like it in the Kali age. It is therefore clear that the passage refers distinctly to the names of the four yugas and their respective standards of virtue.

Two other works, which though of a later date than the Aitareya Brahmana are still Vedic Srutis, refer to these yugas by name. The Mundaka Upanishad (I. 2. 1.) says that "the works, which in the Mantras the seers saw, spread manifoldly in the Treta Yuga;" and in the Gopatha Brahmana (I. 28.) mention is made of one 'Doshapati,' who at the beginning of the Dwapara, is supposed to have acted as the eleventh Rishi.

As has been said above, these names also occur, though in a different sense, in the Taittiriya Brahmana and in the two recensions of the Vajasaneya Samhita in connection with the topic of Purushamedha. Different classes of persons are therein enumerated as appropriate sacrificial victims at the Purushamedha, and in so doing the Brahmana (III. 4. 1. 16.) says: "(Sacrifice) the gambler to the king of dice; the keeper of the gambling house to the Krita; the umpire to Treta; the spectator to Dwapara; and the man, who always remains there like a pillar, to Kali." In both the recensions of the Sambita of the White Yajus (Madhyandina, XXX. 18; Kanwa, XXXIV. 18.) a very similar statement is made. Says Weber (*I. L.* p. 113.) "The names of the three dice (Krita, Treta and Dwapara) in v. 18, are explained by Sayana, commenting on the corresponding passage of the Taittiriya Brahmana, as the name of the epic yugas, which are identical with these—a supposition which will not hold good here, though it may, perhaps, in the case of the Taittiriya Brahmana." But it is clear from the contexts that, neither in the one case nor in the other, the words denote anything else but the names of dice. This is also the opinion of Muir, who says: "In both places they denote dice, as does also the word Krita in Chhandogya Upanishad IV. 1.4."

In one of the parables of this Upanishad, one flamingo is reported as having said to another regarding one 'Raikva with the car':—"As (in a game of dice), all the lower casts belong to him who has won with the Krita cast, so whatever good deeds other people perform, belong to that Raikva." A little further down (IV. 3. 8.), the following statement occurs:—"Now these five (the eater Vayu, and his food Agni, Aditya, Chandramas and Apas) and the other five (the eater Prana, and his food speech, sight, hearing and mind) make ten, and that is the Krita (the highest) cast. Therefore in all quarters those ten are food (and) Krita (the highest cast)." To understand the force of these passages one must first know the nature of the game of dice then in use. Even now a game exists, which is played with two pieces of wood, or of ivory, or of brass, each about an inch long and having four sides, one side of which being marked with 6 dots and the next three with 4, 3 and 1 dot respectively. These two pieces are held in the palm of one's hand and rolled on to the ground. The number of dots on the side turned topmost indicates the number of points gained by the player, which regulates the motions of certain pawn-like pieces on what nearly resembles a chess board. The game referred to in the Upanishad seems to have been a little different. The dice was then, as Griffith says, made of the nuts of the Vibhitaka tree, and the four sides seem to have been known by the names of Kali, Dwapara, Treta and Krita, and to have been marked in order with one, two, three and four dots on the four sides of the piece. If the player succeeded, when rolling the piece on to the ground, in making the Krita side with four dots turn up topmost, he appears to have thereby scored the largest number of points, namely, ten, which is the total number of all the dots on the piece (4 + 3 + 2 + 1 = 10).

The meaning of the first of the passages quoted above from the Upanishad is that just as the person who succeeds in making the gambling piece turn up with the Krita side topmost scores ten points, that being the total number of dots of the four sides thereof, so also Raikva's good deeds are so vast and varied that the merit of others also goes to him, *i. e.*, accounts for nothing in the eyes of the public before the grandeur of his merit. The other passage denotes that Vayu, as Vayu, absorbs the four others and, as Prana, swallows up the four senses during sleep. These ten are said to be the Krita cast, which has already been said to swallow up the lower casts and thus secure ten points to the winner. "Therefore," says our Upanishad, "in all quarters (which are ten, including Zenith and Nadir), those ten are food and Krita." Says the commentator Sri Sankara, "Thus those numbers (4, 3, 2 and 1) making up ten constitute the Krita cast. Since this is so, therefore, in all the quarters, fire etc. and speech etc. are the food,— because of the number ten being common to both." So much explanation of this obscure passage is enough for our present purpose, which is to show that, according to the Upanishad, the gambling die was marked in order with 4, 3, 2 and 1 dot on its four sides.

There is a passage in the Taittiriya Brahmana (1. 5. 11.), which also uses the names Krita and Kali in a similar sense. In recommending that only four *stomas* (eulogistic verses) should be used in the Jyotishtoma sacrifices, it says: "That in which there are four stomas is Krita, then that in which there are five is Kali; therefore there must be only four stomas." Now if it be remembered that the Kali side, containing one dot, adjoined the Krita side with four dots, it becomes clear that after the Krita comes the Kali side, and not a side with five dots. As analogy very largely served the place of argument in the days when the elaborate disquisitions of the Brahmanas were being put in shape, in order to prove that there should be only four stomas, recourse was had to the gambling die, each point of which was fancifully compared to a stoma. The largest number of dots on any one side having been only four, the stomas also were not to exceed that number.

Thus it is evident that in the Taittiriya Brahmana, Vajasaneya Samhita and Chhandogya Upanishad, these words are not used, as in the Aitareya

Brahmana, to denote the yugas bearing those names, but rather signify the sides of a gambling piece. What then was the original signification of these words? To take up first the words Krita and Treta, they appear to me to have originally meant 'the fourth' or 'four,' and 'the third' or 'three' respectively. Krita and Treta are derived from the same roots as the Latin '*Quartus*' and '*Tertius*'. In Sanskrit dictionaries the word Krita is taken also to mean 'four', a signification which dates from the earliest times of Aryan history and which must not be supposed to have recently arisen in India from the circumstance that the Kritayuga is the fourth prior yuga, consisting of four times the period of the Kaliyuga. The word Kali is generally derived from the root '*Kal*,' to count; and very probably the number one was originally, as now, known also by that name. Just as now in India, when a person is asked in the vernaculars to count the numerals, he is generally told to 'Say one, two,' so that the first of the numerals sometimes does duty for the process of counting, so also the word Kali, denoting one, might have given rise to the idea of counting signified by the root '*Kal.*' Besides, if we remember that the first side of a die marked with one dot was known as Kali and that the third side with three dots and the fourth side with four dots were named Treta and Krita respectively, it becomes clear that these three words were originally only numerals.

The word 'Dwapara' has a different story. On its face, it is a compound of two words 'Dwa' and 'para.' If a person, acquainted neither with the names of the yugas nor with those of the casts of dice, were to be asked to interpret the word, he would unhesitatingly say that it meant '*the second para*,' for that is the literal, and, I may also say, the original signification. It will be shown in a subsequent chapter that in the early Vedic times, there existed a cycle of one thousand years, which was probably known also as '*Para*,' and that two such cycles had intervened between the epoch of Ikshwaku and the beginning of the Kali-yuga. If '*Para*' was therefore a duration of 1000 years, the word 'Dwapara' must have meant 'the second period of 1000 years.' In the opinion of the late Taranatha Tarka Vachaspati, Dwapara is so called because it came after (*para*) the first two (*dwa*) yugas: द्वाभ्यां (सत्यत्रेताभ्यां) परः द्वापरः॥. Thus, according to either of these interpretations, the word Dwapara is a term decidedly belonging to the nomenclature of the Chronology of Ancient India.

It is not perhaps generally known that gambling was once the besetting vice of the Kshatriya community in India. The Epic tells us many stories of kings having been ruined by this fatal game, notably of Nala and Yudhishtira, both of whom, however perfect they might in every other respect have been, proved to be extremely susceptible to the allurements of dice. So disastrous had it come to be to the welfare of the Aryans in India even in the very earliest times, that a great Rishi, Kavasha Ailusha by name, stood up to earnestly oppose it. The force and the persuasiveness of the preaching of this ancient Reformer is revealed to us in a fine hymn* of fourteen verses, wherein he graphically depicts the hollow pleasures and the real dangers of this questionable pastime. When this kind of gambling had attained firm hold in Aryavarta, each of the four sides of the die came to be known by the name of the number of dots on it, or in other words, by the names, Krita, Treta, Dwita† and Kali. When the idea of the four yugas subsequently took shape, the word 'Dwita,' the name of the side marked with two dots, might have given place to the word 'Dwapara.'

* Rig Veda, X. 34.

† This word was well-known at the time, as it occurs many times in the Rig Veda, though in a different sense.

It was about the time of the War that the yuga system had first come into existence, for these four yugas, as we have seen, are referred to for the first time in the Atharva Veda Samhita and in the Aitareya Brahmana. As has been remarked above, it will be duly proved in another chapter that a real historical period of two cycles of 1000 years each, dating from the epoch of Ikshwaku, the son of Vaivasvata Manu, came to an end a few years after the Mahabharata War. At this time there were also vague recollections of a pre-historic age preceding the epoch of Ikshwaku. This was probably the first age of the Gods (*Devanam Prathama Yuga*), referred to in the Rig Vedic hymn (X. 72. 2), a period lost in mist and stories of deluge.* Thus there were three distinct ages or yugas preceding the War, namely, the two historical cycles of 1000 years each and the mythical age before the times of Ikshwaku.

There was still another age which commenced soon after the war and which was made to last for 1000 years on the analogy of the cycle of 1000 years which came to a close at that time. This yuga, which was then current, was the first or the 'Kali' age; and

* Taittiriya Samhita, VII. 1. 5; Satapatha Brahmana, 1. 8. ; VII. 5. 1. 5 ; Kathaka Samhita, XI. 2.

the immediately preceding age was already known by the name of 'Dwapara'. The next prior age, which, according to the Puranas,* commenced at the time of Ikshwaku and Pururavas, the progenitors of the Solar and Lunar dynasties, was named as the third or the 'Treta' yuga; and the earliest mythical times, preceding the time of Ikshwaku, was the fourth or the 'Krita' yuga.

An historical period of 2,000 years having come to an end soon after the War, the Dwaparayuga seems to have been confounded with the whole of that period; and the Kaliyuga was supposed to last, as we have already seen, for a period of 1,000 years. If the preceding Dwapara, which was the second age, was to last for 2,000 years or double the period of the Kali, it followed as a matter of course that the Treta or the third age should last for thrice that period, or for 3,000 years, and that the Krita or the fourth yuga should extend for a period of 4,000 years. Moreover the number of dots on the Krita, Treta, Dwapara and Kali sides of a die were four, three, two and one respectively. It is probable that the difference in the periods for the four yugas was also due to the analogy of this model.

* Bhagavata, IX. 14. 49.
See also Ramayana, Uttara Kanda, Ch. 74; Warren's Kala Sankalita, pp. 358 and 366.

Lastly, I shall briefly refer to the views* of Professor Rangacharya on the subject. He considers that the Kritayuga was so named, because it was an age 'of deeds,' "when everything that had to be done was done as a matter of course."† I submit that this is a secondary signification, which subsequently came sometimes to be attached to the word. Such fanciful interpretations do occur in many of our ancient writings like the Brahmanas, the Mahabharata and the Puranas; but instead of having been meant to give the historical origin of the words explained, they were merely used to drive home the full force of the words in all possible and fanciful aspects. As has been said above, the words Krita and Treta were originally numerals derived from the same roots as the Latin *Quartus* and *Tertius*, and are therefore similar in origin to the names of the Geological Epochs, *Quaternary* and *Tertiary*. Mr. Rangacharya interprets 'Dwapara' as 'doubt or philosophy', and 'Treta' as 'a collection of threes'; and says that the Yugas were so called because the Dwapara was an age of philosophy and the Treta was the yuga when the three fires of sacrifices, the three castes and the three classes of gods were, according to the

* The Yugas, pp. 35, 36 and 42.
† *Vide* also Mahabharata, III. CXLIX. 12.

Puranas, supposed to have come first into existence. Without discussing the fatal questions whether the Treta yuga was really so considered at the time when these names came into being and whether the Dwapara means, or actually was, an age of philosophy, I shall be content with briefly pointing out that both the Parasara and Manusmritis attribute the exactly contrary characteristics to these yugas.

तपः परं कृतयुगे त्रेतायां ज्ञानमुच्यते ।
द्वापरे यज्ञमेवाहुः दानमेकं कलौ युगे ॥*

"Spiritual meditation predominates in the Kritayuga and spiritual knowledge in the Treta. They say that sacrifice only prevails in the Dwapara and that liberality alone survives in the Kaliyuga." If Manu, which most scholars place before the beginning of the Christian Era, may be expected to hand down the old traditions more or less faithfully, we find that the leading characteristic attributed to the Dwapara is not 'philosophy,' but sacrifice, and to the Treta, is not 'sacrifice,' but knowledge, the exact reverse of Mr. Rangacharya's contention. Moreover, it may also be remembered that the greatest Hindu lexicographer of our times, the late Taranatha Tarka Vachaspati, interprets the word Dwapara in a quite different manner.

* Parasara Madhaviya, I. 23; Manusmriti, I. 86.